JAGUARS FOR THE ROAD

BY HENRY RASMUSSEN

JAGUARS FOR

Published by Motorbooks International,
Publishers and Wholesalers, Inc.,
Osceola, Wisconsin, U.S.A.
Copyright 1985 by Henry Rasmussen.
ISBN 0-87938-188-4.
Library of Congress number 84-22704.
Printed in Hong Kong by
South China Printing Company.

THE ROAD

After a decade of building sidecars for motorcycles and coachwork for plain automobiles, William Lyons was ready to move on to other things. In 1934 he hired William Heynes; the styling talent of Lyons, mated with the engineering skill of Heynes, produced a sensational sports car: The SS 100.

Its beautiful body was of aluminum and attached to a structure of ash. The frame was a box-section type with half-elliptical springs front and rear. The engine was an in-line six, obtained from Standard. With Harry Weslake, Heynes designed a new cylinder head, featuring pushrod-operated overhead valves. Carburetion was handled by two SUs. The four-speed synchromesh box also came from Standard. The knock-offs were 18 inches tall; the wheelbase 8 feet 8 inches; the weight 2,680 pounds.

Only 308 were built between 1936 and 1940; 190 of a 2 1/2 liter version, 118 of a 3 1/2 liter. The former produced 102 bhp and a top speed of 94 mph; the latter, 125 bhp and 101 mph. Zero to 60 took 11 seconds. The Lyons formula was already at work: outstanding styling, performance to match, all at an incredibly low price: only 395 pounds Sterling; 445 for the 3 1/2 liter.

During the war, with his factory now building bomber components, Lyons found time to plan for the future. Production of prewar saloons was resumed already in 1946; Heynes, now joined by William Bailey and Walter Hassan, again teamed up with Weslake to construct an all-new in-house power plant.

In the meantime Lyons finalized the styling of the future models. The new engine was primarily meant to power a new saloon, but, with his typical flair for publicity, Lyons decided to introduce it in a new sports car: The XK 120 was born.

It caused a sensation when shown in 1948. Lyons made plans for a 200-unit run, the body to be made in the same expedient way as before, aluminum over ash. The frame was a shortened version of the one used in the saloon. Suspension was by wishbones up front and half-elliptical springs at the rear. The in-line six had double overhead cams and produced 160 bhp. Two SUs handled breathing. Zero to 60 took 12 seconds. Top speed was an incredible 125 mph, making good the company's claim that the XK 120 was the world's fastest sports car. It could be had for the most reasonable sum of 3,945 dollars. Lyons had done it again!

SS 100

XK 120

With demand for the XK 120 so great, it was decided to start large scale production. A total of 242 aluminum Roadsters were built before the pressed-steel units became available in 1950. In 1951, a beautiful Fixed Head Coupe was added to the line, and, in 1953, a Drop Head Coupe. Altogether 7,612 Roadsters were produced; 2,678 Fixed Head Coupes; 1,765 Drop Head Coupes.

The XK 140, built between 1955 and 1957, was changed in several areas: sturdy bumpers front and rear, altered grille, chrome strip down the rear lid. But more importantly, it had increased power: 190 bhp. Also, the engine had been moved forward, creating more space in the cockpit. Rack-and-pinion steering was yet another important improvement. The wheelbase stayed 8 feet 6 inches. Overall length increased by 3 inches, to 14 feet 8 inches. Weight was up by 200 pounds, to 3,100. In spite of that, 0 to 60 took 11 seconds; top speed increased to 130 mph.

Momentum was maintained! Altogether 3,354 Roadsters were built; 2,808 Fixed Head Coupes; 2,889 Drop Head Coupes. Value for money spent was still extremely high; the luxuriously appointed Drop Head Coupe sold for 3,810 dollars.

The XK 150, introduced in 1957, was improved and restyled. It retained the basics of its predecessors, the XK 120 and the XK 140. Esthetically, the new model had lost some of its good looks. Functionally, however, it was superior; front and rear windows were now wraparound, improving visibility; the cockpit was wider, resulting in a more comfortable interior.

At first only the Coupe was available. In its basic form, it had drum brakes and the 190 bhp engine. The special equipment version had wire wheels, twin exhaust, twin foglamps and, significantly, Dunlop disc brakes as well as the blue top 210 bhp engine. The next year saw introduction of both the Drop Head Coupe and Roadster models. The latter also came in an S version, which meant the gold top engine, producing 250 bhp and a top speed of almost 140 mph. Zero to 60 took just 8.5 seconds. The cost had risen slightly; 4,763 dollars in 1960.

By 1961 the incredibly succesful XK 120, 140, 150 series had run its course. Of the XK 150, 4,462 Coupes had been built; 2,671 Drop Head Coupes; 2,265 Roadsters. All in all, since introduction in 1949, 30,504 units were put on the road.

XK 140

XK 150

While sports car sales proved strong, Lyons saw even greater potential in high-performance luxury saloons. The Mark V, built from 1947 to 1951, was a holdover from the prewar era. It had, however, received a new chassis. In 1950, this chassis was mated to the new XK engine. Enveloped in a new example of Lyons' styling talent, it was introduced as the Mark VII.

The body was of pressed steel. The chassis had wishbones and torsion bars up front, and half-elliptical springs at the rear. Steering was servo assisted. Brakes were drums. The engine produced 160 bhp. An automatic transmission came in 1953.

In 1957 the bulbous shape needed slimming: The Mark VIII, while basically unchanged, received a sweeping chrome strip on its side panel and two-tone color scheme. A curved one-piece windshield improved looks. It also had more power: 190 bhp.

In 1959 came the Mark IX, with disc brakes and power steering. The 210 bhp gave a top speed of 120 mph and a 0 to 60 time of 15 seconds—all in the comfort of sumptous leather and walnut; all at the affordable price of 3,850 dollars. A total of 47,190 units (all three versions) had been built by 1961.

With a sports car and an up-market saloon in production, Lyons concentrated on a more compact sedan. Introduced in 1955, the 2.4 was the first in a series of variations. Its success would earn Jaguar a place in the big league. At the end of the road, in 1969, a total of 145,000 units had been built.

The 2.4 was the first unit-body Jaguar. Wishbones with coils were used up front; trailing-links with cantilever springs at the rear. The engine was a smaller version of the XK, producing 112 bhp. The 3.4 came in 1957. It sported a 210 bhp engine and 120 mph. Disc brakes came in 1958. For 1960, the same basic model, now called Mark II, was updated again: Suspension changes improved handling, wider rear window made for better vision, new dash improved safety. Also available was the 3.8, with a 220 bhp engine and a top speed of 125 mph.

In 1967 the basic car was still around, now called the 240 and the 340, depending on engine. After the merger with British Leyland in 1968, only the 240 remained. Price of the low-end model at introduction was 2,400 dollars. Thirteen years later, inflation had done surprisingly little damage—just 200 dollars.

MK IX

MK II

The XJ, introduced in 1968, was perhaps the best sedan design ever by Lyons. Although modern, it had classic Jaguar lines. Underneath, it had more tradition: the proven XK engine—now reduced to 2.8 for the European market; for the US market (from 1970) it kept the 4.2 size, producing 245 bhp, a 0 to 60 figure of about 10 seconds, and a top speed of 120 mph.

The front suspension had been redesigned to include antidive geometry. Power steering was standard on the 4.2. As a first for a Jaguar sedan the XJ had rack-and-pinion steering. Disc brakes were used all around. Both manual (until 1979) with optional overdrive and automatic was available.

The XJ came in a variety of disguises: The two first model years are unofficially referred to as Series 1. With the introduction (1970) of the XJ-12, came the Series 2. Also available at this time was the L: the long wheelbase. Its popularity led to eventual elimination of the short wheelbase. In 1974 came a facelift: slightly higher roof, new grille, bigger bumpers, new rear lights, etc. This is Series 3. The XJ is Jaguar's all-time bestseller. To date (1984 included), around 400,000 units have been built.

XJ6

Lyons knew the value of racing victories; already from the beginning the XK 120 broke speed records, excelled in rallying and placed on top in outright circuit events. The C-Type, developed from the XK 120, won at Le Mans both in 1951 and 1953. The D-Type took the formula one step further; this, one of the all-time greats among sports racing cars, gave Jaguar three more Le Mans victories: in 1955, 1956 and 1957.

While the C-Type was built around a space frame, the D-Type was of a monocoque design. Attached to its central section, with its bulkheads, was a tubular frame, holding engine, front suspension and front section of the body. Rear suspension was attached directly to this center section, as was the rear portion of the body. Power source was the proven 3.4 XK unit, fed by three Webers. Output was 245 bhp. Zero to 60 took just 4.7 seconds. Top speed was 160 mph, plus. A new Jaguar-designed gearbox, disc brakes and rack-and-pinion steering were other features.

A total of 71 units were built. About a dozen were factory team cars, with the rest going to privateers. The official list price was just below 10,000 dollars.

D-TYPE

If the SS 100 was William Lyons' first masterpiece, and the XK 120 his second, then the E-Type was his third. But while the two others had been clever interpretations of the general trend among sports cars at the time, the E-Type was as original as it was ingenious. Much of the credit for the shape must go to Malcolm Sayer, who had also styled the D-Type.

The engineering was also inspired by the D-Type, although transmission and engine came from the XK series. The power source was the 3.8 unit used in the S version. It produced 265 bhp, and propelled the new Lyons creation from 0 to 60 in 7.1 seconds. Top speed was a very healthy 150 mph.

The basic ideas of the monocoque construction, as used on the D-Type, were carried on to the new sports car, as was the front suspension and the outboard front-wheel disc brakes. In the back, the E-Type went two steps further; for the first time, Jaguar now had independent suspension, and the disc brakes were placed inboard for less unsprung weight.

After four years of development, the new Jaguar was first shown at the 1961 Geneva Salon. It caused a sensation!

E-TYPE 1

The first-version E-Type, built between 1961 and 1968, is commonly referred to as Series 1. Of the 3.8 Roadster (61-64), 7,827 were made, and of the Coupe, 7,669. In 1964 came the 4.2. In addition to a larger displacement, it also had an all-synchromesh gearbox, as well as a better clutch, and improvements in the cooling and electrical systems. By 1968, another 9,548 Roadsters and 7,770 Coupes had been built. In 1966 came the 2+2, the first to be available with automatic transmission. By 1968, 5,598 units had been built of this version, fixing the total number of Series 1 E-Types put on the road at 38,412.

In 1968 the Series 1 1/2 made its debut. The changes were mainly in appearance: The rake of the windshield was increased and the headlights lost their attractive plastic covers.

The Series 2 came in 1969. Most features were the result of the changing character of sports cars; the emphasis now had to be on comfort as well as safety and emission laws. The E-Type received stronger bumpers, new rear lights and changes to the interior. During its two-year production run, 8,627 Roadsters, 4,855 Coupes and 5,326 2+2 Coupes were built.

E-TYPE 2

With the arrival of the Series 3 E-Type, came changes of a drastic nature. Mechanically, the new model was built on a longer chassis, the same as used for the 2+2, and had therefore grown more than six inches in overall length, creating more room in both engine compartment and cockpit. Overall width had also grown, by 2 inches, as had height, also by 2 inches.

But the most significant new feature was the V-12 engine. It had a displacement of 5.3 liters, was fed through four Zeniths and produced 272 bhp in European guise. Performance was back! Zero to 60 took just 6.4 seconds, and top speed was 146 mph. Regrettably, for the US market the trend was reversed: In 1972, the engine produced 250 bhp; in 1974, 241. Zero to 60 now took 7.4 seconds and top speed was 135 mph.

Visually, too, something had been lost—the sacred proportions had been tampered with. Of the Series 3 2+2 Coupe, built between 1971 and 1973, 7,297 units were put on the road (the two-seat coupe was no longer available). Of the Series 3 Roadster, built from 1971 to 1974 (a few in 75), 7,990 were produced. The last fifty units were painted black—the E-Type era was over!

With the passing of the E-Type, enthusiasts wanted a replacement. But, when the XJ-S came in 1975, it was not what they expected. In fact, judging by the standards Jaguar helped define so well, it was hardly a sports car at all. It fell into a category between a sports car and a luxury sedan. Nevertheless, the XJ-S was an outstanding creation. It performed extremely well in its areas of designation: comfort, sophistication, elegance.

The new car was based on the technology found in the XJ sedan. It had the same chassis (but with a shorter wheelbase) and the same front and rear suspensions. Power came from the 5.3 liter fuel-injected V-12, giving 285 bhp in Europe. Zero to 60 took 6.7 seconds (manual). Top speed was 150 mph plus. In the US, as always, the figures were not as good. Output was 244 bhp, 0 to 60 took 8.6 seconds (automatic), top speed was 137 mph. Price at introduction was 19,000 dollars. In 1985, the new HE version was priced at 36,000 dollars.

By 1979, 13,729 units had been built. Sales in the US dropped to just a few hundred in 1980 and 1981, then surged at an incredible rate: In 1984 alone, 3,480 units were sold.

E-TYPE 3

XJ-S

A BREED APART

Automobiles, like animals, come in a variety of breeds, their individualism noted as much for the way they look, as for the way they work. But, unlike their counterparts in nature, automobiles are created by men—sometimes many men, sometimes only a few.

Enzo Ferrari is most often thought of as the great inspirator. He did not himself design an engine, a chassis or a body; he chose the men who could—great engineers like Gioacchino Colombo. Ferrari provided the vision and formulated the goals. To fulfill the vision for the shape of his automobile, he chose Pinin Farina. The Ferrari became an amalgamation of the genius of these men.

Ferdinand Porsche was himself a great engineer. He passed this ability to his son, who, using his father's work as a basis, gave birth to the Porsche breed. But while the anatomy was Ferry Porsche's, the shape came from another hand, that of Erwin Kommenda.

William Lyons, the father of the Jaguar, stands unique among his peers. Not only did he inspire great achievements from engineers like William Heynes, he also created the looks of his automobile. In that sense the final product carried his mark to the degree of Ettore Bugatti, the greatest of automotive artists. And, in that sense, Lyons, too, was an artist. Also, like Ferrari and Porsche, Lyons was an entrepreneur, a businessman with the vision and talent to build and manage an industry.

Lyons was an inspirator, an artist, an industrialist, all in one—a breed apart.

I wish this book, however inadequate in format and scope, to be a tribute to Sir William Lyons, and to the sports car he fathered, the Jaguar—also a breed apart.

Henry R.

O ld or new, at rest in front of battered garage doors or posed on the open road, the lines of a Jaguar are always striking. The SS 100, pictured to the left, epitomizes the evolution of the open sports car of the late thirties. Seen above, the Mark IX, Jaguar's luxurious top-of-the-line choice in the early sixties. To the right, the XJ-S, Jaguar's contribution to fast motoring in the style of the eighties.

Decay contrasts luxury. Filthiness contrasts spotlessness; an old railroad depot, its corrugated-steel front rusty and warped, certainly brings out the beauty of the freshly restored XK 140 Drop Head Coupe, seen in the photographs to the left and right. In the picture above, the strong, smooth lines of the Mark II are effectively contrasted with the slender skeleton of the Howard.

One could hardly accuse a Jaguar of being extravagant. Opposite page, far left, the first badge to include the famous feline features was the one displayed on the XK 120. After thirty years it is still pristine. Beside it, top, the badge attached to the cam cover of an XK 140. Below it, the cat decorates the grille of an XJ-6. On this page, above, it reappears on an E-Type, and, to the near left, on an XK 150. Notice that the word Jaguar is no longer part of the design on the latest badges.

Shown on these pages, pictures of the eyes of the animal. Opposite page, far left, the headlights found on the XK 120. Featured next, the twin units of the XJ-S. Its shape was a compromise to comply with US laws; the European version had a distinctive, single-beam design. In the case of the E-Type, a compromise was again required; the picture to the near left, shows the smooth cover of a Series 1, and, above, the compromise, as it appears on a Series 3. To the far left, the rear lights of the XK 150.

Wheels, while of course primarily practical in purpose, have often been the object of decoration. Pictured to the far left, the wire wheel of an XK 140. Next to it, that of an SS 100, and, above, a Series 1 E-Type. Wire wheels were, to begin with, an option. Also in the beginning, while available chromed, they were just as commonly painted. Pictured to the near left, the wheel of a Mark IX. This is the same unit used on the XK 120; pressed steel, with separate beauty ring and hubcap.

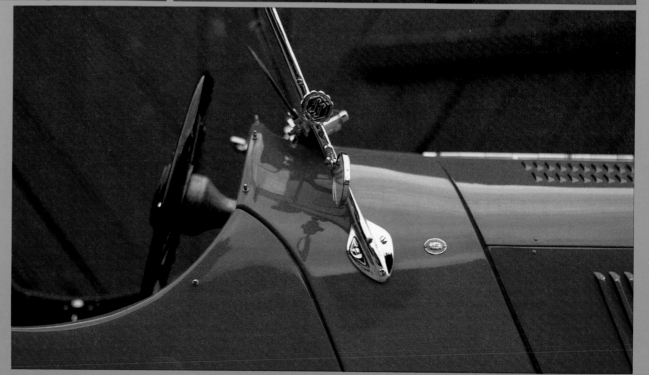

Supporters of open air motoring found in Jaguar a car whose cockpit expressed a unique combination of down-to-business and, forgive me, comfy-cozy. In an SS 100, pictured to the right, one sat out in the open to an extreme degree. The fold-down windscreen and the low-cut doors saw to that. The XK 120, top, right, provided only slightly more protection. In the D-Type, above, the driver sat well enclosed, a necessity when shooting through the air in excess of 160 mph. To the left, the cockpit of the Series 1 E-Type.

Meaningless decorations were never a part of the Jaguar interior. A purely functional simplicity, as seen in the SS 100, opposite page, near right, and in the XK 120, above, became even starker in the D-Type, to the right. This unsentimental approach to design was carried on to the E-Type, opposite page, bottom. Even when elegance was called for, as in the XK 140 Drop Head Coupe, far right, it was always done with prudence and discrimination.

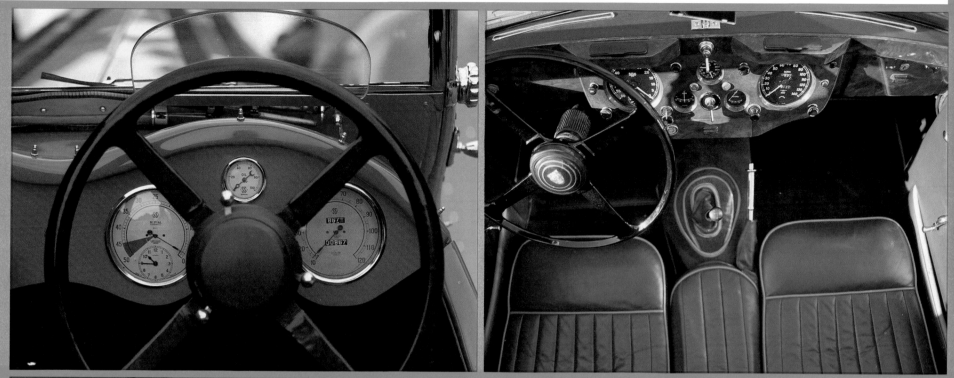

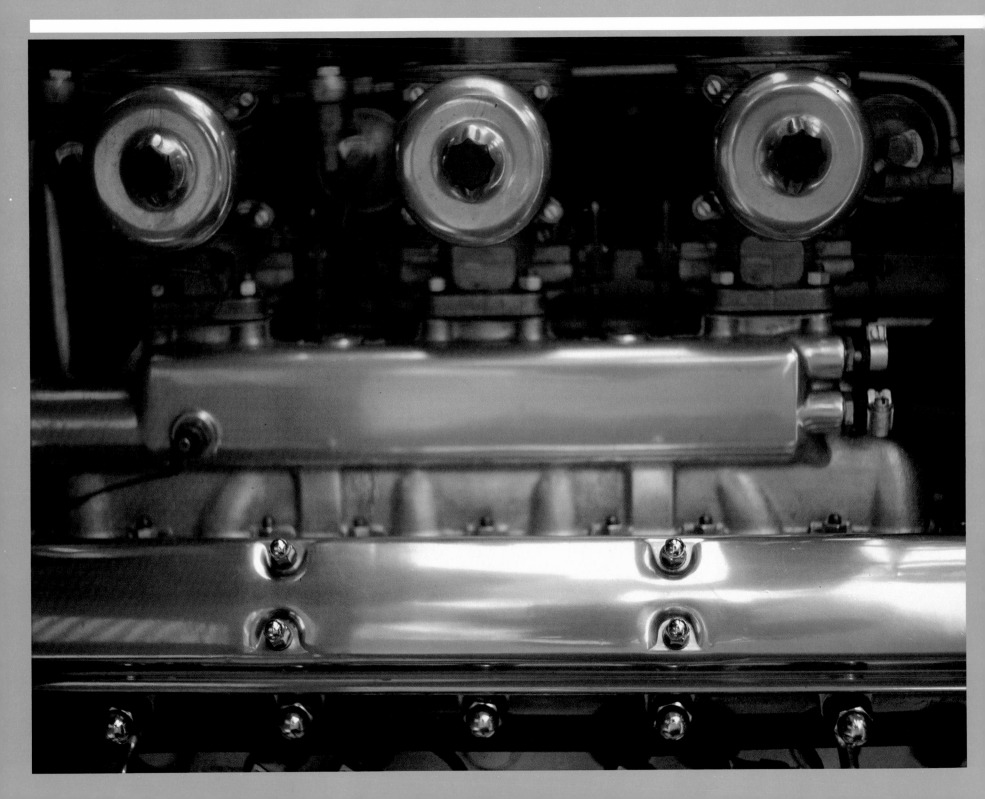

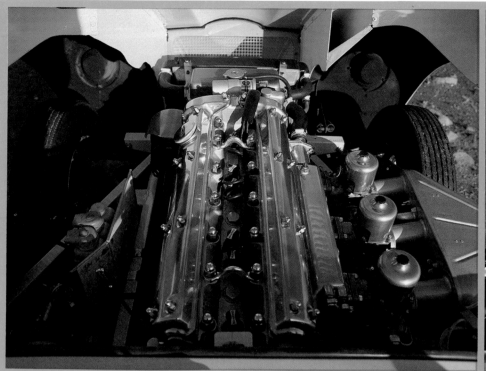

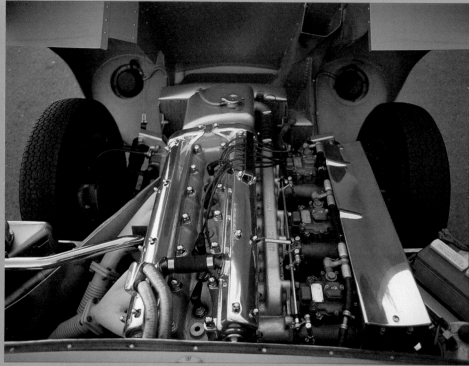

Under the skin of a Jaguar beats a strong heart. Engineered much like a prewar Grand Prix engine, it was just as competent on the track as it was on the road. To the left, a bird's-eye view of the XK-engine as it looks mounted in a Series 1 E-Type. Just how closely related to the D-Type it was, becomes evident when comparing the two pictures above: the E-Type to the left, and the D-Type to the right. To the lower right, the V-12 as mounted in an XJ-S. Esthetically, as well as mechanically, simplicity had given way to complexity.

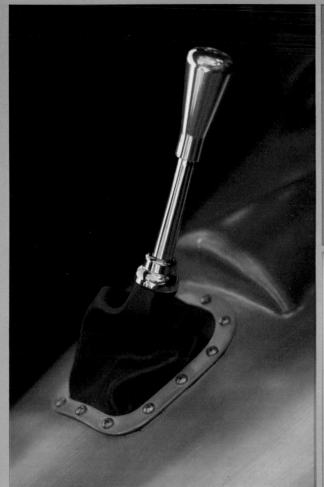

Dictated by the simple logic of function, the appearance of the details take on a special beauty. This seems to be more true with a Jaguar than with many other cars. Study the shift lever of the D-Type, its combination leather strap and handle, as well as the row of louvers on the hood of an E-Type. Even when a different kind of beauty is desired, Jaguar excells; study the touch of Sir William Lyons as it is expressed in the window and dash of a Mark IX.

Owners of Jaguars tend to possess a unique character which blends mechanical aptitude with a romance for the automobile. On this spread, a sampling of Jaguar enthusiasts. From left to right, top to bottom: Jason Len, owner of XK-Unlimited, a parts and restoration business in San Luis Obispo, California, prefers a Mark IX for the road, and a modified E-Type for the track. Judith and Robert Gillette, of Long Beach, California, own three Jaguars which they both work on and play with—the perfect husband-and-wife team.

From behind the wheel of the latest XJ-S, Chic Vandagriff, owner of Hollywood Sport Cars, Hollywood, California, reflects on his many years of involvement with Jaguars, both as a dealer and as an enthusiast. Ron Laurie, of San Francisco, California, enjoys the view from the cockpit of his D-Type, which he is not content to just pose in, but drives with gusto in vintage racing events. Ed Rouhe, of Riverside, California, normally found behind the wheel of one of his Ferraris, is seen here sampling the competition.

SS 100

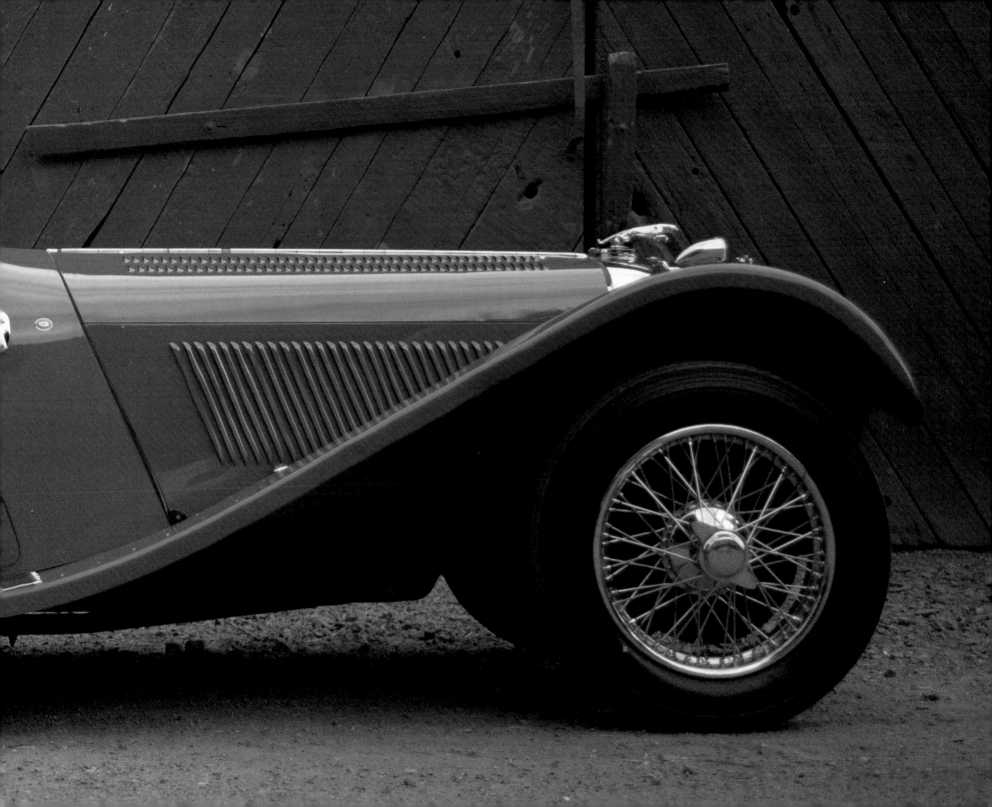

A TOUCH OF LYONS

The rejuvenation of the British sports car, like most changes in that island kingdom, was slow in coming. As late as the mid-thirties, the essence of this archconservative breed was still exemplified by marques like the HRG and the Frazer-Nash. Their unimaginative lines certainly brought out the fact that the creators placed no great emphasis on styling. There were, however, winds of change in the air.

These currents of innovation came from Italy, where Carrozzeria Zagato had given sensually flowing lines to the Alfa Romeos of the early-thirties. The beauty of these machines could hardly be ignored; their photographic images adorned the pages of the motor magazines as they reported on victories from all over the Continent. In 1930, the assault of the Alfas reached the home front: The legendary Nuvolari and his 6C 1750 were the winners of that year's RAC Tourist Trophy race.

The Italian influence was most evident in the Riley RMP of 1934. Sweeping lines could also be seen in other British cars of that period—in the Hillman Aero Minx, for instance, and in the handsome, but shortlived, Squire.

The most successful of these stylish new sports cars, however, was the one conceived by William Lyons. It was designated the SS 90, and had long fenders, flamboyantly arched over the wheels, and rounded tail, incorporating gas tank and spare wheel. Unfortunately, only the prototype received this beautiful rear. The production version was fitted with the conventional slab tank and upright spare wheel. Nevertheless, the way the rear fenders terminated in big-radius curves was enough to tie front and rear together, giving the new sports car a most fashionable look—a look that would become classic in its own right.

Not yet a Jaguar, the SS 1 was nevertheless Lyons' first attempt at building his own car. The engine, however, was still supplied by an outside firm—a Standard straight six with a two-and-a-half-liter displacement. As with all future creations by Lyons, the styling of the SS 1 was advanced. And the fashionable lines could be enhanced by a wide choice of colors—trendy new shades, such as apple-green and carnation-red. The example seen in these unique pictures was found in Argentina. The model year is 1932, the only year for this version. About five hundred units were built.

Another twenty-two SS 90 units were built before the SS 100 was introduced in September 1935. This version had the same basic appearance as the SS 90, but was a true 100 mph car. While the Squire, for instance, had a price tag of 1,100 pounds Sterling, and the Riley cost 550, the Jaguar—as it was now called, for the first time—could be had for only 395.

The principles of Lyons' success formula—distinguished appearance, outstanding performance, attractive price—had been displayed in a most convincing manner.

I have just succeeded in squeezing behind the wheel of the red SS 100 parked in the warehouse used as temporary storage for some of the cars in the Blackhawk Collection. Now it's a matter of folding my right leg in such a way that it can join the rest of my body. It proves to be easier said than done. However, after several tries, the task is accomplished.

Now the small door, hinged in the suicide manner, must be closed. This task, too, requires several tries. Once completed, however, all is fine and dandy. Or is it? How does one get out? I find that it would be reassuring to know, and, investigating the action required, I realize that the small knob cannot be reached—not by performing any of the traditional movements. Finally, by squeezing my left arm between my abdomen and the steering wheel, I'm able to reach that all-important little knob.

Reassured, preparing to settle down again, I discover that there is no room for my right arm; it has to hang out across the edge of the low-cut door. It suddenly dawns on me that this tradition sprung from dire necessity rather than a desire to look nonchalant.

Now, having settled these practical matters, I find that, instead of feeling irritation, I have derived a primitive pleasure from it—an emotion heightened when I look out across the large steering wheel, out beyond the curved eyebrows of the dashboard, out through the small Brooklands screen, out across the long hood,

(continued on overleaf)

Caught in these photos, the car that first brought William Lyons to the attention of the sports car world, the famous SS 100. This 1937 Survivor, chassis number 39002, was the second one built of the 3 1/2 liter version. First scheduled for delivery to John Black, director of the Standard Company, it now belongs to the Blackhawk Collection in Blackhawk, California.

on out to the tip of those outrageously tall fenders. After passing over the silver Jaguar that leaps fearlessly from the crest of the radiator, my gaze returns to the right fender, follows its smoothly sinking line as it dips below my elbow and vanishes into the blur of the spinning rear wheel...

The director of the Blackhawk Museum, Donald Williams, has graciously agreed to let me photograph this Survivor. He has recently obtained it from Steve Sim Roberts, who supplied me with its history.

The chassis number is 39002, and it was the second unit to be built of the 3 1/2 liter version, as well as being the oldest surviving example of that type, since 39001, the first unit, delivered to Prince Michael of Rumania, is believed to have been destroyed during the London blitz.

Number 39002 was originally reserved for John Black, director of the Standard Motor Company, supplier of engines for the Jaguar cars. For some reason, Black did not exercise his option. The car instead went to C. C. Bellhouse of New York City. It was the first of only three or four believed to have been originally sold to the United States. Later records show the car to be the property of T. Hecht in Georgia. In 1973, G. Daigh of Atlanta had become the new owner. He restored it from the frame up, and did it so well that the car, after a string of Best in Class and Best of Show, was awarded the coveted National First Place Grand Classic by the Classic Car Club of America.

As I place my hands on the steering wheel, preparing to guide the sleek machine through the open warehouse doors, out onto the narrow road that winds in and out between golden California hills, I finally have to face up to the illusion: I'm not going to be able to sample the real thrill of this Survivor—the gearbox is out for repair. Like most other enthusiasts, I have to be content with the illusion, for it is only afforded a lucky few to have experienced the true excitement of an SS 100.

The SS 100 was the first to carry the Jaguar name—and the model destined to bring the company its first dose of fame. The unique curve of the fenders always makes it easy to recognize, whether, as in the 1939 photo to the left, parked in front of the factory or, as in the 1967 photo above left, posed with its top raised. Above, a peak under the hood. The remaining two pictures feature radio and television personality Dave Garroway at Bridgehampton in 1950. To the right, he is fighting to bring the rear back in line. To the upper right, he has completed the spin. Trying to get back on track, he has caused the engine to overheat—the day is lost!

XK 120

THE REAL THING

Now, when I see the setting again, I realize there is something mystical about it, like in a place of worship. It has to do with the moss-covered trunks, with the light that sifts through the layers of leaves, with the narrow road that widens just here, and then disappears in a diffusion of foliage. But more than that, it has to do with the XK 120 itself, parked at the roadside, resting there like an image of some long-forgotten jungle god.

I had chosen the setting on instinct, without the car. And now, seeing the XK 120 in place, I'm convinced I was right.

But, was I right in choosing this particular car? It's so plain, so gray. People are used to bright colors, red, yellow. They want to see chrome, reflected in the sun. They want to see wire wheels, spotless leather. The concourse scene has spoiled their tastes.

This XK 120 is the way it was when new. It has never been tampered with. Never been repainted. Of course, never been restored. It never had to be. It has gone only twelve thousand miles! It is new! Actually, better than new. It has the patina that comes with age, the charm and the beauty of an antique.

I wonder why people are so eager to take all that away. So quick to paint, so quick to rechrome, to reupholster, to redo...

When the war was over, and it was again time to build sports cars in England, inspiration for the new fashion in body styles, came from the Continent, as had also been the case with the new trends in the early-thirties.

It is safe to assume that William Lyons was familiar with the creations of the Italian carrozzerias. It is possible that he had seen, at least in

the form of a photograph, the one-off Alfa Romeo roadster Pinin Farina built in 1940. It had an all-enveloping body; its front and rear fenders consisted of one unit that arched across the front wheel, curved down to a low point at cockpit level, then rose again above the rear wheel, which was covered by a skirt.

However, if Lyons in fact never saw this Alfa Romeo, he could most certainly not have missed the highly successful BMWs. These machines were also very advanced in the field of aerodynamics. In the 1940 Mille Miglia, besides campaigning the winning Touring-styled coupe, the BMW team fielded two roadsters. With the benefit of hindsight, it is interesting to see how much they resemble the XK 120 of eight years later. Incidentally, these two roadsters were styled by Manfred Kempter in Munich, working under the auspices of the government of the Third Reich.

In addition to the possible Italian influence on Lyons, it also seems likely that he was inspired by the French coachbuilders. In 1938, at Earls Court, Lyons displayed a beautiful, streamlined coupe version of the SS 100. It reveals a definite kinship to the 57 SC created by Jean Bugatti. The coupe was regrettably never placed in production, but it was a clear indication of the direction of Lyons' thinking. Traces of the future XK 120 are clearly evident in this coupe, especially in the treatment of the rear, with its long, sweeping lines and skirted wheel.

How did William Lyons do it? What was the creative process? Unfortunately, very little concerning this vital subject is mentioned in Jaguar literature. Author Paul Skilleter claims that the XK 120 was hatched during a two-week period, immediately preceding the 1948 London Motor Show. According to this account, Lyons, as was apparently his habit, collaborated with a team of panel beaters, who, interpreting his instructions, worked directly in aluminum, directly on a chassis, directly in full size. Were there no sketches? No models? How could such perfection of line be arrived at using as obstinate a

(continued on overleaf)

Lyons' milestone creation, the XK 120, made its sensational debut in 1949, first in roadster form, above left, then in 1951 in coupe form, above. Both were photographed at the Geneva Salon, the coupe in 1952, the roadster in 1953. Left, a car that might have influenced Lyons and his XK 120—one of the aerodynamic BMW roadsters prepared for the 1940 Mille Miglia. It was restored by one of the great preservators of vintage BMWs, Jim Proffit, of Long Beach, California. Right, proof that the popularity of the XK 120 reached the far corners of the world—a most beautifully restored coupe belonging to an enthusiast in Australia.

With lines that seemed more French than English, William Lyons stunned the sports car world when his XK 120 was unveiled in 1948. This 1953 Survivor, chassis number 673029, belonging to Thomas Kreid of Rancho Santa Fe, California, is unique in a sense that it is virtually brand new; with 12,000 miles on the odometer, nothing ever needed to be done to it.

medium as metal? It requires a sure eye. And a sure hand.

The reference to the creative forces that seem to have influenced Lyons is not intended to take away from his genius. After all, his creation was not a copy. Even if he did, like so many others, follow a trend, his contribution was beyond those of his peers. Study, for example, the termination of the roofline on the 1951 XK 120 Coupe! Lyons, with one bold stroke, took this line to perfection!

Just as with the SS 100 of the mid-thirties, Lyons, in the XK 120, managed to capture the essence of the trends of the period, creating yet another classic in the process.

The owner of this virginal XK 120, Thomas Kreid, wants me to drive it. He isn't hesitantly agreeing to let me drive it. No, he insists that I drive it! He insists that I drive it hard, so I can feel and know what this car is really about. After all, its looks are only one aspect.

I'm sitting high, but still not far above the floor. The massive body out there is round and smooth. The steering wheel is large and close to my chest. I accelerate out of the first curve, registering the surge in exhaust note, fierce and resonant, registering the sound of gravel thrown onto the fender wells by the spinning wheels. Going through the curve, I feel a curious motion. Is the tail sliding? Or is it my imagination? It is a good feeling.

Out on the paved road I push the XK 120 harder through the curves. And I realize that the good feeling comes from the car bending with the road, turning with the curve, flexing its muscles, like an animal in motion...

I chose this car on instinct. Now I know I was right. Although worn and corroded here and there, every nut, every bolt, every stitch, every clamp in this machine is the original one, tightened and fitted by the original craftsmen in Coventry. This is not a rebuild: Not the result of an effort to come as close as possible to the original. This is the real thing!

On these pages, photographs of the XK 120 in its natural habitat—the roads and tracks of competition and speed record events. Above left and right, American devotees battle the elements in their quest for victory. Above right, a classic Jaguar photo, capturing for posterity the scene on a Belgian highway in October of 1953. The specially tuned and prepared XK 120 Roadster has just set a new record for the flying mile, reaching an incredible two-way average of 172 mph. Posing proudly for the photographer are driver Norman Dewis, in goggles; racing manager Lofty England, far left; stylist Malcolm Sayer, fourth from right.

XK 140

COMPARING APPLES

Irvine is a fast-growing community in Southern California, a shining example of successful city planning. Twenty years ago, its fertile soil supported only a few scattered buildings and acre upon acre of fruit trees and vegetables. Today, almost all this has been taken over by housing developments.

In one spot, however, where the railroad once stopped, stand forgotten remnants of the past—a post office, a packing plant, a collection of buildings in a state of decay—a perfect place to contrast the beautiful with the ugly.

Along the length of the railroad tracks, separated by a row of tall palms, stretches a gigantic monster of corrugated steel.

The sun is about to rise. Its first warm light touches the corrugated wall, painting it orange. Below this band of flaming color, surrounded by cold, predawn shadows, stands a light-blue XK 140 Drop Head Coupe.

Inside this space of time, lasting only a few minutes—while shooting and scrutinizing the car from every angle—I'm overcome by a feeling I experience only on rare occasions, at particular times, in particular places, in the presence of particular cars. I recall the moment on a dock by the Hudson River, as the sun set behind the tall towers of the World Trade Center, when the sensual body of a 1936 Cord Sportsman, creme colored, disappeared between cranes and containers. And I remember the time in the desert behind the San Bernardino mountain range, at dawn, when a Gullwing, bright red, its doors poised for flight, was first touched by the morning light.

It's my subconcious telling me when I'm con-

fronted with a masterpiece...

Dennis Terry has been a Jaguar enthusiast for years. He once owned an XK 140, a coupe, but it had to be exchanged for the necessities of life. A few years ago, when things had become comfortable, the urge returned. He began searching for another Jaguar, this time his favorite body style, the drop head coupe.

In 1981 he spotted an ad in the Los Angeles Times: 1956 Jaguar, XK 140 DHC, C-engine, overdrive, wire wheels, 56,000 miles, one owner, $4,900. It belonged to Helen and Ralph Baker of Newport Beach. After a quarter of a century, during which time the Jaguar had been one of their dearest possessions, they knew the car had to be passed on to someone else, someone who could restore it to its original splendor, for, over the years, it had regrettably decayed. Even washing and polishing had become too much of a chore for the elderly couple.

The Terrys found the car to be complete, but the exterior had been repainted in a nonoriginal color, and the interior was worn to beyond recognition of original shade. They wrote the factory, who willingly supplied the delivery specifications of the car. The color had been Pastel Blue; the interior, dark blue with light blue piping, the top, also dark blue.

At the end of 1984, after three years and a succession of restoration firms, the XK 140 stood completed. But it had not happened without trials. For instance, one of the individuals involved in the restoration managed to lose the window frames. They seemed impossible to replace, but after a search that even took him to England, Dennis finally located a new set in Arizona. The installation of the engine as well as the final touches to the car were performed by Ray Sanchez in his Costa Mesa service and restoration shop.

Although this example of the XK 140 is one of the finest around, the Terrys have no intention of entering the show circuit. To own it, to look at it, and to drive it once in awhile—very early on

(continued on overleaf)

Featured on top of the left-hand page, two views of the XK 140 Roadster. While the shape of the body shell was identical to its predecessor, the revised model sported a new grille with fewer and wider bars and new bumpers of substantially greater weight and strength. To the lower left, the XK 140 Coupe. This version, because of its enlarged cockpit, had lost some sleekness, but gained some roominess. Captured above and right, two American pioneers of sports car racing—sports columnist McCluggage, in her Drop Head Coupe, and restauranteur Sardi, in his Fixed Head Coupe.

Growing up, for the XK 120, meant turning more civilized. It got heavy bumpers, new grille, roll-up windows, together with other changes of a cosmetic and comfort nature. It was now called XK 140. Pictured in these photographs, a 1956 Drop Head Coupe, chassis number 818031. It was purchased from its first owner by Edna and Dennis Terry of Costa Mesa, California. With input from the Jaguar factory, it was recently brought back to its original splendor.

weekend mornings—is enough.

The shooting session is over. And the sun has risen. As I watch the XK 140 drive off I can't help but feel a tinge of possessiveness. Its lines express all the elegance and nostalgia of the classic two-seater touring machine. It is indeed one of the most beautiful and well proportioned designs I've ever seen. My mind begins to build an imaginary situation, finally confronting me with a question. If you could own three of the nine cars in the XK series, which ones would you pick? I see them lined up in front of a three-car garage that looks suspiciously much like the old granite marvel belonging to a moneyed friend of mine in Connecticut.

The first to go is the XK 140 Coupe. Its greenhouse is too large, once you have seen the perfect proportions of the XK 120 Coupe. Next to get the slip is the XK 150 Coupe, also overshadowed by the original one. Since I must have a closed car in my line-up, the 120 Coupe is the first finalist. Next to go are the XK 120 and XK 150 Drop Head Coupes. Influenced by the car I have just seen, I feel the XK 140 is the most beautiful. The heavier bumper is not disturbing. It actually serves to dress up the car more formally. In its XK 120 form, the design of the bumpers made the car look naked, which, of course, was perfect for the racing look. So, the second finalist is the XK 140 Drop Head Coupe. For the last spot, it's a matter of choosing among the roadsters. I decide on the XK 150. In its S-configuration, it's the fastest of the XK series. And the lines of this model, with its long, smoothly swept rear deck, and its bold, aggressive stance, are seductively attractive.

I've chosen an example of each of the models and body styles. And, as I visualize the three in front of the garage of my imagination—the one that regrettably does not resemble my own—the silver coupe with tan interior, the blue drop head coupe with dark blue interior, and the white roadster with red interior, make for a darn good selection. But, please, don't ask me to narrow the list to one!

The venerable XK was one of the most versatile, long-lived and formidable engines ever produced in large quantities. In addition, it was one of the best looking. Seen in the pictures on these pages, it is fitted in a variety of vehicles, covering the spectrum from sports racing to luxury saloon. Powering the 1951 C-Type, above, it produced 200 bhp. Pulling the 1955 2.4 compact sedan, left, it gave 112 bhp. As fitted in the 1959 XK 150, near right top, it was available in a range from 190 bhp to 250. Powering the 1964 3.8, far right top, it produced 220 bhp. In the 1961 E-Type, lower near right, where it was mounted in the manner of the C- and D-Types, it produced 265 bhp. Finally, as seen in the picture to the lower far right, it is fitted in the 1962 Mark X, producing 245 bhp. It surely is one of the best looking sedan engine compartments of modern time.

XK 150

OF FATE AND FORTUNE

Blackpool, 1919. Imagine the young William Lyons. See him in his father's music shop, eighteen years old, bright and determined, but still not displaying obvious signs of greatness. He had not excelled in school. He had not shown interest in a profession. In fact, only one subject seemed to occupy his mind: motorcycles. Oh, yes, there was also this constant talk about wanting to start his own business!

Actually, as fate would have it, his first job had indeed been in the automotive field. But his apprenticeship with Crossley in Manchester, a renowned manufacturer of both engines and complete automobiles, lasted only a short time. He was soon back in Blackpool.

However, fate had yet another lesson in store for young Lyons. It was as a junior salesman in a local car dealership. A high point of this period came when the company sent him to London to work the auto show. Thus, more by coincidence than by design, in 1922—twenty-one years old—William Lyons had gained valuable experience in the automotive business, both in manufacturing and in merchandising.

Now fate brought a fellow motorcycle enthusiast, William Walmsley, in his path. Walmsley had designed a sidecar for his own use. Its looks were so striking that he had been encouraged to build a small series.

This was the chance William Lyons had been waiting for! He immediately recognized the commercial possibilities, convinced Walmsley to become a partner, obtained starting capital,

rented facilities and hired help.

The Swallow Coachbuilding Company, as the outfit was originally called, prospered under the determined leadership of Lyons. In 1927, the company took an important step forward, introducing a pretty little streamlined car, built on the Austin Seven chassis. A string of such specials followed, using Morris chassis, Standards, Wolseleys—even Fiats—all fashionably styled and reasonably priced.

Business was so brisk that larger facilities were needed; only two cars a day could be handled in the original plant. The move to Coventry came in 1928. However, the company was still just a coachbuilder, and Lyons indeed had greater ambitions. In 1931, Swallow introduced two cars of its own design, the SS I and the SS II. Both chassis and engines were still built by an outside firm.

The success of these models propelled the company into a spiral of continued growth. The next few years saw introduction of improved and restyled versions of the SS I and II, as well as a radically styled Airline saloon. Further milestones along the way to becoming a full-fledged car manufacturer came in 1935 and 1937, with, initially, the SS 90 and SS 100 sports cars, then, with the first steel-bodied saloons.

By 1927, the name of the Swallow organization had been changed to Swallow Sidecar and Coachbuilding Company. By 1935, in connection with becoming a public company, the firm was renamed SS Cars Limited. The initials stood for Standard Swallow or Swallow Sports, no one knows with certainty which. By this time William Walmsley had left the organization.

At the outbreak of World War II, William Lyons could look back on nearly two decades of progress. Before the plant had to be modified for wartime production of bomber components, the company had reached an annual production of more than five thousand units.

Yet, it was only the beginning!

The XK 150 Coupe rolls slowly down the nar-
(continued on overleaf)

Jaguar's presence was felt far and wide during the early postwar years of racing. In the photo to the lower left, Jorge Caamano is showing off his mount during a 1951 race in Mendoza, Argentina. Captured to the upper left is a scene from the start of the Mille Miglia. The year and car are a mystery. Could it be a Biondetti XK 120 Special? The styling appears to be C-Type inspired, which would fix the year at 1952 or 1953. The C-Type shown in the photo above represents just one of the dozen examples seeing action on American soil. Even Jaguar saloons got into the action. To the right, German Peter Lindner handles his 1957 3.4.

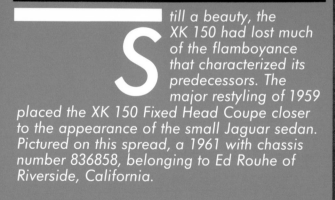

Still a beauty, the XK 150 had lost much of the flamboyance that characterized its predecessors. The major restyling of 1959 placed the XK 150 Fixed Head Coupe closer to the appearance of the small Jaguar sedan. Pictured on this spread, a 1961 with chassis number 836858, belonging to Ed Rouhe of Riverside, California.

row road, orange groves on both sides. The owner of this freshly restored beauty, Ed Rouhe, sits beside me in the cockpit, looking very British in his sports cap. The exhaust noise flows gently through the open windows. This particular car is equipped with the optional Borg-Warner automatic transmission, engaged via a lever on the dashboard.

Everything about the XK 150 expresses the changing priorities the Jaguar company in the late fifties. These changes were dictated by in-house planning as well as a new trend in the marketplace. While the XK 120 had initially served as a springboard for Jaguar, catapulting it right to the very top among sports car manufacturers, the spectacular racing victories that later followed with the C- and D-types, had eliminated any further need for racing development. Furthermore, the tastes of the broader segment of sports car enthusiasts had changed, away from a fascination with the primitive to an emphasis on the comfortable.

All this was reflected in the XK 150. Thus it was both less exciting and more acceptable. It had improved visibility and more room. It even had small seats in the back. Stylingwise, it retained the Jaguar look, but it had lost the arrogant sleekness. From an engineering viewpoint, it was definitely improved. It could be had with all-around disc brakes. Also available was the S-type engine, with 265 bhp.

Going so slowly on the narrow road, constantly registering the differences in this model, as compared to its predecessors, I was beginning to feel disappointed. Was this just another promenade car? But, I should have trusted Sir William. I should have realized that he would never let an enthusiast down. Turning out on the 91 freeway, heading toward Riverside, I let my heavy foot sink to the bottom of the pedal, and low and behold, that familiar exhaust note was still there, vibrant with Le Mans nostalgia, and that power and speed was also still there, resplendent with Monthlery and Monte Carlo romance... I was reassured, the XK 150 was still all animal—all Jaguar.

While the basic style of its predecessors, the XK 120 and the XK 140, had been retained, the updating of the new XK 150 had quite obviously caused the loss of much of the famous sleekness of those early cars. The widening of the cockpit, as well as the smoothing-out of the dip in the waistline, were some of the chief causes for this change in appearance. Nevertheless, the XK 150 was still a beautiful machine. The Drop Head Coupe, above, looks rather elegant in a light color and whitewall tires. The same set of features are equally effective on the Fixed Head Coupe, seen in the two pictures to the upper right. Most exciting of the three versions, however, is the Roadster, pictured to the lower right. There is a particularly pleasant relationship between the long hood, the small top, and the sloping tail. Regrettably, all the variations had lost the wooden dash, left.

MK IX

MARK OF A MASTER

The outbreak of World War II marked the end of an era. This was certainly true of the way the war affected virtually every aspect of life and society. It was certainly also true as far as it concerned SS Cars Limited.

During the war, William Lyons took advantage of the break in automotive production to formulate plans for a new line of cars, plans that encompassed every aspect of car manufacture, from styling to marketing.

After the war, the new era was initiated by the adoption of a new name. Obviously, the old SS initials were no longer acceptable, bringing to mind one of Hitler's most hated institutions. The company, from then on, would be known as Jaguar Cars Limited.

Already in 1945, postwar production was resumed with only minor changes to the prewar saloon. It took three more years before the automotive world would know what Lyons and his men had really been up to during those long nights on firewatch.

The first phase of the plan was not spectacular. It came in the form of a new chassis. Then, a restyled version of the saloon, designated Mark V, appeared. As was soon apparent, this car was not meant to be a part of the new line-up. It was merely a transitional model.

The second and third phases, however, implemented in 1948, were truly spectacular. They came in the form of a new engine, the first wholly designed by Jaguar, and a new sports car, the sensational XK 120. The engine, on which work had begun already in 1943, had really been conceived for a new big saloon, a corner-

Immediately after the war, or as soon as the factory had been cleared of the bomber components manufactured during those years, Jaguar resumed production of a saloon, above, which was virtually identical to the one built just before the war. While the factory referred to it by the size of the engine—1 1/2, 2 1/2 and 3 1/2 liter—enthusiasts often call it the Mk IV. To the left, Clark Gable is seen behind the wheel of a three-position Drop Head Coupe. In 1948 came the Mark V, its richly appointed interior and its smoothly curved exterior, seen to the right. Seen above it, the Drop Head version.

stone of Lyons' plan. This saloon, designated Mark VII, was introduced in 1951.

Thus, in the mid-fifties, all the elements of the plan had been implemented. They covered the full spectrum of the luxury market, from a sports car—available in a variety of body configurations—to a compact family-oriented saloon, to a luxury saloon with limousine options.

This frontal assault, so brilliantly executed, and so splendidly supported by spectacular racing successes, is a textbook example of automotive marketing warfare, as well as a showcase of William Lyons' genius.

The ultimate result of this plan, translated into production numbers, was staggering, especially considering the humble beginnings. Altogether, more than a quarter of a million units were put on the road, placing Jaguar in the big league of automotive manufacturers.

Like so many times before, for the sake of catching that perfect light, I find myself standing by a wayside at dawn. On this occasion, the road is winding its way up a hill from which I would have been able to see the waves of the Pacific, had it not been for the forest of a peculiar species of windswept eucalyptus. On the other side of the road, between my camera and the rising sun, stands a white Mark IX, its opulent form slowly becoming exposable. Jason Len, the owner, sits behind the steering wheel, waiting, as I do, for the right moment to begin the shooting of the car.

Jason had bought the car a few years ago in Studio City. The seller was an agent, acting on behalf of an aging moviestar. Jason found the Mark IX parked under a tree. The sunroof had been left open, exposing the interior to the weather; the leather had deteriorated to beyond salvation; the wood was cracked and faded. On top of that, the engine was apart, its various elements thrown about, left to corrode. The car was a basket case—just what Jason had been looking for: something to occupy dead time in his shop.

(continued on overleaf)

Bentley and Rolls-Royce, watch out! Here comes Jaguar! In Mark VII, Lyons had a winner. Not only did it do just about everything just as well as the competition; it cost a lot less. The Mark IX featured here, chassis number 793184, the property of Jason Len of San Luis Obispo, California, was the last of the series. This 1960 example came with both disc brakes and automatic transmission.

Jason had always been drawn to cars. At an early age, his mother remembers, young Jason placed a D-Type at the top of his Christmas list. Later, in his early teens, most of his free time was spent helping a neighbor keep an old TC running. At the age of twenty-one, he opened the doors to his own service and restoration shop, specializing in British cars. In 1975, the business was expanded to include a mail-order department. Today, XK's Unlimited is a factory-authorized purveyor of Jaguar parts, and has customers all over the world.

Jason's areas of enthusiasm, however, are not limited to servicing and restoring Jaguars. He also races them. Presently he is campaigning a highly modified 1963 E-Type Series I Coupe. The rear end is from a Series II, and the brakes from an XJ-S. Using technology not available during the heydays of the C- and D-Types, Jason has been able to extract approximately 375 horses from the 4.2 engine, while revving it as high as 7500 rpm. During the first season, competing in events at Riverside and Willow Springs, success eluded him. There are still many shortcomings to be sorted out, he says. Watch me next season!

The light is perfect now, the sun illuminating the sky, but not yet showing above the horizon. While shooting the Mark IX, studying its styling at the same time, I realize that the shape of this big saloon is actually an adaptation of the ideas expressed in the XK 120, an expansion of the same forms, in this case made wider and taller and longer for the sake of roominess. The same swelling fenderline is there, as is the dip ahead of the rear wheel, the skirt, the roof line, and the curved rear quarter window. Only for the purpose of a more formal look did Lyons choose the upright grille.

While a bit rotund, the Mark IX is a perfect expression of the opulence still to be found in cars of the early postwar years. The big saloon, magnificent in the morning light, looks as rich and inviting as the bosom of an operatic prima donna. I decide I'm very attracted to it.

The Mark VII, introduced at Earls Court in 1950, was an amazing car. Not only did it have the understated exterior elegance and sumptuous interior accommodations normally found in an exclusive limousine—making it proper transportion for a discriminating English gentleman—it also had the handling and performance characteristics of a sports car—making it a machine he could have won races with on the weekends, although such activities would most surely have been deemed improper. Actually, some gentlemen did go racing—a Mk VII walked away with the top honors of the 1957 Monte Carlo Rally. In 1956, an upgraded version, the Mk VIII, was announced, and in 1958 came a further improved version, the Mark IX. The exterior differences between the Mk VII, seen on this page, and the improved versions, opposite page, are easy to find—but spot the differences between the VIII and IX!

MK II

PASSION PERPETUATED

In most cases—referring to styling—the original design seems to be better than any later attempts to modify and update. For instance, the early short-nose Ferrari 275, as opposed to the later long-nose version, in my opinion, displays a better balance between front and rear. And the second-generation Porsche 356 Coupe B, with its raised lights and bumpers, did not look as good as the original Coupe A.

This axiom, however, does not apply to Jaguar's compact saloon, the 2.4 and 3.4 models, introduced in 1955.

In this design, Lyons seemed not quite up to his usual mastery. While the overall look indeed was a continuation of the Jaguar tradition—the front and rear displaying obvious XK 140 heritage—the dip in the fenderline was gone, so that front and rear were now connected in one sweeping curve. This was a new approach. It was, however, not a negative one. It gave the new design a modern look, even adding a sense of aerodynamic efficiency.

Actually, where the new design fell short was in the attention to details, an area where Lyons had always excelled. The window pillars on the new saloon were quite heavy, which gave the car a somewhat ungraceful look. Also, the rounded rear side window, a Lyons trademark since introduced on the XK 120 Coupe, had disappeared. In its place was a rather uninspired shape, made worse by a rain channel that continued the line downward.

These shortcomings, however, cannot be blamed on Lyons. The compact saloon, as a complete package of body engineering and de-

sign, was the most complex ever undertaken by Jaguar. For the first time, unit construction was used. This new method was still not fully developed, and many areas of the body were kept generously rigid, giving up styling considerations rather than taking a chance on encountering future stress problems.

The first changes came two years into production. The grille was made wider, anticipating that of the XK 150. Also, the solid skirt used on the original design, was now cut down, alleviating much of the weighty look.

The second set of revisions to the styling came in 1959, with the introduction of the Mark II. The window portion of the doors were now no longer part of the pressing. Instead the windows received slim frames, smoothly sculpted and chromed. Also, the rounded rear side window was back. With the glass section chrome-framed, this area became a highly decorative element. Enlarged front and rear windows also helped to eliminate the old heaviness.

With these changes in place, the Mark II embarked on a seven-year journey, during which it received a number of subtle modifications. This period constituted a high point.

If the beginning of this model was a low point—still in reference to styling—it also ended in a low point; in 1967, the 240 and 340 models were introduced. The attractive bumper design of the original model was now replaced by a simpler and cheaper version. And, as a link in a chain of austerity measures (if one can use the word austerity about any Jaguar), the interior was now vinyl instead of leather.

In 1961, one of the cars from the high-point era, equipped with the top-of-the-line 3.8, 220 bhp engine, was delivered to a banker in San Francisco by the name of Clarence Baumhefner. The beautiful new saloon was black, as befitted a member of this exclusive group. Baumhefner was a consumate car enthusiast, and entered the Jaguar in that year's Concourse de Elegance at Pebble Beach.

The model featured to the left, introduced in 1955, and simply named after the two engine options available, was William Lyons' entry into the more compact category. The 2.4 had a narrower grille than the 3.4, as illustrated by the photograph at the top of the left-hand page. The photos on this page, from the top, show the Mark II 3.8, introduced in 1959. Notice the very effective redesign of the glass area. The basic body style was Jaguar's bread and butter for more than a decade. The last versions came with the 240 and 340 models, shown in 1967. The 340 was only available for one year, while the 240 lasted two.

(continued on overleaf)

Words like quality and quantity were key elements of the Lyons success formula. Its validity was proven by the phenomenal popularity of his small saloon, here shown in its 1960 Mark II guise. Although it was not your average family sedan, to the owner of this particular Survivor, Bob Baumhefner of Sepulveda, California, the words family sedan, take on a very special meaning. Bob's father bought the Mark II, chassis number 213392, brand new. Recently he presented it to his son, with the understanding that it would always stay in the family.

On display in the Baumhefner family album is a black and white Polaroid photograph showing the Jaguar parked on the famous Pebble Beach lawn. The black surface of the car is alive with reflections. Its chrome is exploding with sunbursts. The front license plate carries the word Jaguar in the best British fashion. It all reflects pride of ownership. Posing beside the car is son Robert, in his early teens, and his younger sister Bonnie. Their excited smiles reflect the importance of the occasion.

The family album also contains another photograph, taken the same day, with a different camera—one belonging to Robert. It features the Jaguar by itself.

The next decade saw the Jaguar used as an everyday car. In its owner's mind it was always, regardless of age, an automobile to cherish and treat with special care. This attitude was transmitted from father to son.

Another entry in the album shows the car on a particular day in 1971. Robert, at this point attending medical school, had given it a thorough wash and wax job. The result deserved a series of pictures. They focus on the car alone, featuring it from a variety of angles.

In 1974, Robert was ready to begin his career. As a graduation gift, his father presented him with the Jaguar. It was understood that it would always stay in the family.

By the following year, 1976, Robert had completed a thorough detailing of the Jaguar, and had enough confidence in the car to enter it in the Jaguar Club Concourse at Bush Gardens. His faith was rewarded with a first in class. An inscribed silver tankard signified the honor. An entry in the album shows the trophy placed on the hood of the Jaguar.

The latest entry in the Baumhefner family album captures the Jaguar on the tarmack of the Santa Paula airport. In addition to the car, posed beside a classic airplane, the picture shows a bearded fellow in the process of photographing the Jaguar mascot.

Incidentally, Robert has a son of his own now. His name is Adam.

The S-Type Saloon, opposite page, top, was first shown in 1963. Based on the Mark II, the new model had an enlarged trunk area. In 1966, it received a different grille, center picture, and was now referred to as the 420 Saloon. Pictured to the lower left and above, is the Mark X, introduced in 1961. This was the largest and most luxurious Jaguar ever made. In 1966, this model became the 420G. The plain 420 production run ended in 1968, while the 420G was made until 1970. The two photographs to the lower right, are sufficient proof of the plushness of the Mark X series.

CROWNING ACHIEVEMENT

In the life production of a great painter, there often seems to be one particular masterpiece that captures the essence of his work—instantly recognizable symbols such as da Vinci's Mona Lisa and Picasso's La Guernica.

Although industrial design is not thought of with the same reverence as fine art, there is a similarity in impact; Le Corbusier's Grand Confort armchair and Loewy's Coldspot refrigerator, come to mind.

The genius of Sir William Lyons is most often connected with other fields of endeavor, such as manufacturing and marketing. Nevertheless, he made a distinguished contribution as an industrial designer. In fact, his achievements in this field may very well be the most long lasting. After all, the impact of the visual reaches the greatest depths of the mind.

Lyons' most important contribution to sports car design, must be the XK 120. A majority of enthusiasts would vote for the roadster, and while this model became the most popular, the coupe was the artistically most outstanding. One must also consider the E-Type. The styling of this model, however, cannot be solely contributed to Lyons, since the shape was arrived at in close collaboration with the company's aerodynamicist, Malcolm Sayer.

Most of Lyons' efforts were concentrated in the area of sedans. Here, his roots go back to the rakish saloons of the immediate prewar and postwar periods. In the early-fifties, he conceived the Mark VII, which, although voluptuous, was both beautiful and dignified. His efforts continued with a compact saloon, introduced in the mid-fifties. And in the early sixties,

The XJ6 was unveiled in 1968. Although the model, at the time, was already recognized as an outstanding design—timeless in its mature simplicity—time has proven the point. Over the years, it has seen a number of more or less subtle changes. Above, a comparison between the 1968 original and the 1972 long-wheelbase versions. The year also saw introduction of the V-12. To the near right, an under-the-hood view. To the far right, the distinctive V-12 grille. To the left, for comparison, the XJ6 grille. Opposite page, top, the rare Coupe, produced between 1974 and 1978. Center, the Daimler Double Six, with its fluted grille surround.

the Mark IX, as the Mark VII had now become, was ready for replacement. It came in the form of the massively rotund Mark X.

In the meantime, the compact line also needed updating. The result was the S-Type, shown in 1963. This model combined the front and mid-section of the Mark II, with a new rear deck. The length was increased by seven inches. Incidentally, the front did receive a few detail changes. Most obvious of these were the hooded headlights and the widened chrome trim around the grille. In 1966, it was time for another facelift. The model was now designated 420, and received a new front that combined a traditional grille with modernistic quadruple headlights, all very much like the front of the 420G, which in 1966 had become the new designation of the Mark X.

The final achievement of Lyons' sedan styling career, and, by many accounts, the crowning act, came in 1968 with the introduction of the XJ6. Just as his creative technique depended on a trial-and-error period before a finished design could be arrived at, the mature, restrained lines of the XJ6 seem to be the grand total of every one of his previous efforts, as if these, too, had just been the trial and errors of the life-long process.

This model also received more or less subtle styling changes. In 1972, a long-wheelbase version was introduced. The four additional inches resulting from this, can be seen in the width of the rear door and window. The original version is the better design. Also in 1972, the XJ12 became available. The only difference was the new grille, which now had vertical slats only, as opposed to the cross-slat design of the XJ6. The XJ12 grille was simpler and, consequently, more attractive.

The following year, a coupe version was unveiled. Personally, not accounting for the rarity of this model, I favor the original sedan. Also that year, came the Series Two version. The bumpers had now been raised, necessitating a shortening of the grille.

(continued on overleaf)

Culmination of the Lyons era, was the XJ Sedan; the hand of Sir William is present in every detail. This 1971 Survivor, chassis number 1L58970, belongs to Ginger Streitenberger of Palos Verdes Estates, California. She and husband Bill happened to see the newly introduced XJ6 at Henley's in London, the classic place to by a Jaguar. It was attraction at first sight. An order was placed; many months later it was ready to be picked up at dockside in New York. A cross-country trip confirmed that the car had more than looks—that first attraction has never faded.

In 1979 came the Series Three. Although quite subtle, the styling changes required extensive retooling. The roof had been raised slightly, and the windshield posts had received more rake, eliminating the frontal vent window in the process. There were also numerous other alterations, too many to detail here, among them a new rear light cluster. The overall facelift, incidentally, was the work of Pininfarina. Although the new look was in some ways improved, as with most attempts to modernize an existing design, the old style remains the most desirable. The same year also saw incorporation of the 5 mph impact bumpers—a definite minus for the looks.

In the spring of 1969, while in London, Bill and Ginger Streitenberger happened to pass in front of Henlys' Piccadilly showrooms. On display was a Regency Red example of the new XJ6. Ginger, especially, was taken in by Sir William's latest masterpiece, and, on her insistence, when Bill again visited London in June, an order was placed.

Had the car come through on schedule, the Streitenbergers would have been the first in their part of the country to own the new Jaguar, but delays caused by smog certification and, more devastatingly, a Long Beach dock strike delayed delivery. The car was rerouted to a Canadian port. Thus, almost two years after the order had been placed, the new owners took delivery in Vancouver.

The Streitenbergers, both long-time members of the Jaguar Owners Club in Los Angeles—Bill, a three-term president, Ginger, a concourse and hospitality chairperson—have shown their prized possession numerous times. A shelf full of trophies testifies to the many successes. In 1980 and again in 1983, their pristine XJ6 was awarded First in Class in the National Championships of Jaguar Clubs.

An automobile conceived with so much love and care, certainly deserves to be maintained in the same fashion. The Streitenbergers are eminently qualified.

In 1979, the XJ design was given a workover by Pininfarina. On the opposite page, top and center, a comparison between old and new. Notice, besides the wheelbase—it had been changed in 1973—the increased rake of the windshield, the elimination of the front window vents, the straightened and raised roofline, among other changes. Also from the rear, Pininfarina's handiwork can be easily spotted—before, left, and after, right. Featured above right, the interior of a 1976 XJ12 Coupe. Above and right, the sumptuous interior richness and the classic exterior beauty of the 1984 top-of-the-line Vanden Plas.

D-TYPE

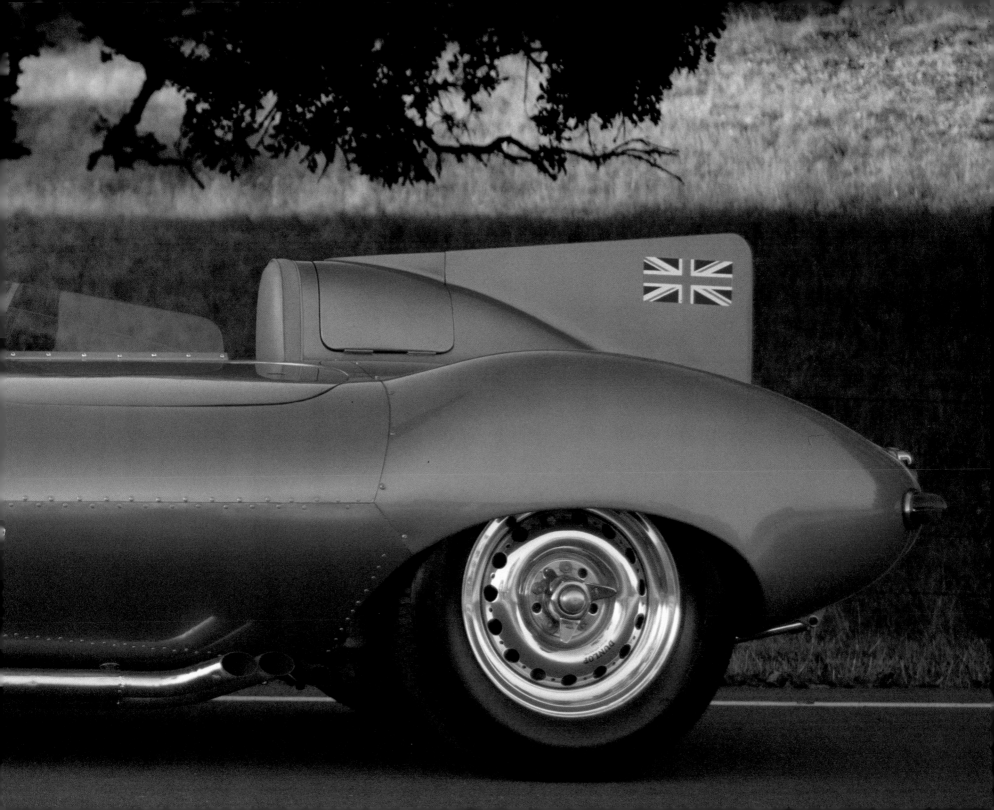

SHAPE OF A WINNER

The 1983 Tourist Trophy Race at Silverstone was marred by apalling weather conditions. This impeded the performance of the drivers as well as the enjoyment of the spectators. Ron Laurie, a Jaguar enthusiast from San Francisco, fared better than most, however; he was a guest in Jaguar's track-side suite.

Recalling the occasion, his memory is dominated by a single image, that of an elderly gentleman watching the race with consumate interest. Significantly, while the other guests had taken refuge inside the covered lounge, with its bar and comfortable chairs, this gentleman—the guest of honor—preferred the solitude of the deck, where only an umbrella protected him from the elements.

In another time, in another place, the same gentleman, William Lyons, could have been observed watching another race. The time was 1950. The place was Le Mans.

Three Jaguars had been entered—privately, for even though the factory had prepared them, it was officially not involved. Lyons had encouraged participation to assess the feasability of future engagement.

Incredibly, Jaguar nearly won the first time out. The XK 120 of Johnson and Hadley, after a slow climb, ran second at the midpoint. With the Jaguar posting faster lap times than those of the leading equipage, there was reason for optimism in the Coventry contingent. Unfortunately, with only a couple of hours left, the car had to be withdrawn due to clutch failure. The two other Jaguars, however, lasted the race, capturing twelfth and fifteenth positions. It was a sensational debut, and Lyons, right there and then—convinced that his machines were cap-

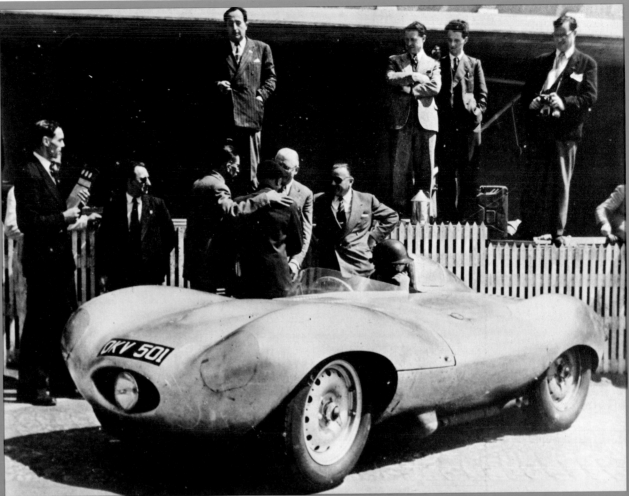

able of winning—ordered the formation of a competition department.

Thus began an era that would leave the Jaguar name deeply engraved in motorsport annals. After a hectic period, filled with the myriad tasks of development and testing, Jaguar's first made-for-racing machine, the C-Type, stood ready for the 1951 Le Mans event—which it won handily.

In 1952, Jaguar showed up with aerodynamic alterations to the C-Type body. There had not been sufficient time to test the effect, and as it turned out, the new nose caused overheating, resulting in the swift elimination of all three cars. In 1953, however, Jaguar was back in the winner's circle, this time after a convincing one-two-four sweep.

For 1954, a new machine had been developed—the D-Type. Unfortunately, in its first outing, this the most formidable of all Jaguars, found itself narrowly beaten by a Ferrari. Then, finally showing its superiority, the D-Type racked up a fantastic string of three victories: in 1955, 1956 and 1957.

When the Jaguar competition department was formed, it was felt that the expertise of an aerodynamicist was imperative. Thus, Malcolm Sayer, previously of the Bristol Aircraft Corporation, joined the organization. The C-Type was his first assignment.

When Sayer's next creation, the D-Type, reached Le Mans—during a rally event that preceded the 1954 race by several weeks—it was still unfinished and unpainted. However, it already had the exciting shape that would win it a permanent spot in the heart of every race car enthusiast.

This shape, although traceable to Touring's 1952 Alfa Romeo Disco Volante, seemed refreshingly new and original. The Alfa, like the Jaguar, had a cross-section reminiscent of that of a flying saucer. The Alfa also had protruding wheel arches as well as head fairings. These fairings were of course not new. They had been

The first hint of what Jaguar had up its sleeve for the 1954 race at Le Mans came during a speed record event at Jabbeke in the fall of 1953. In the photograph to the lower left, can be seen—besides the specially prepared XK 120—the embryo of the D-Type. The next phase was the actual prototype, upper left, pictured during a practice session at Le Mans. Above, the apical D-Type—the long-nose version. Seen to the right, the shape of things to come—had it been allowed come. The V-12-powered XJ13, built with the 1964 Le Mans in mind, would surely have been a worthy successor to the D-Type.

(continued on overleaf)

One of the world's most collectable sports racing cars, the D-Type, looks as brutishly beautiful now as it was savagely successful during its heyday in the fifties. Featured on these pages is a perfectly restored Survivor, chassis number XKD 528, belonging to Ron Laurie, San Francicso, California. Originally sold to a privateer in the United States, it was later owned and raced by photographer Carlyle Blackwell, during which time it was featured in Road & Track.

seen on Formula One cars already before the war, and had in fact been used on several aerodynamic experimentals at Le Mans, notably Cunningham's 1950 Cadillac and Panhard's Tank of 1953.

When the D-Type gained its tail fin, it became truly ferocious looking, although this feature as well, was not new. Vignale's 1947 Cisitalia Coupe, for example, sported twin fins, as did Bertone's 1953 and 1954 Alfa Romeo BAT showcars. In the Jaguar D-Type, however, all these in-vogue elements were brought together to form one of the most effective and pleasing shapes ever to decorate the racing scene—especially in its 1955 long-nose form. A credit to the talent of Malcolm Sayer.

Ron Laurie, our observer from the Jaguar suite at Silverstone, owns an outstanding example of the D-Type. The chassis number is XKD 528, one of eighteen imported new to the United States. It first belonged to Pearce Woods, owner of Continental Motors in Whittier, California, who ran it in local club events. During this time the car was featured in a Road & Track test. In 1956, it was purchased by photographer Carlyle Blackwell of Hollywood. A real sports car enthusiast, he not only raced it, but used it on the street as well. While in his possession, XKD 528 scored its most prominent victory, winning the six-hour endurance race at Pomona in 1958. The drivers were Blackwell and Ken Miles. While owned by Blackwell, the car was again a feature car in Road & Track.

From Blackwell the D-Type first passed to Gary Levitt, then to Joel Finn, then to Howard Cohen. Incurring a fender bender in the historic races at Monterey, Cohen decided on a ground-up restoration. Grisvold's in Berkeley, California, was selected for this task. Upon completion, XKD 528 was sold to Laurie, who has continued its racing tradition.

In 1984, this exceptionally beautiful machine was awarded the Jaguar Salute Trophy at the Santa Barbara Concourse. The D-Type, once a winner, always a winner.

Those were the days! The picture above, from 1956, shows the D-Type featured in this story, while owned by Carlyle Blackwell. When did you last see an all-out race car gas up at your friendly neighborhood station? Seen to the far right, the XK unit as fitted in the Blackwell car. To the near right, the fuel-injected unit of a factory team car photographed at Le Mans in 1956. On the opposite page, ultimate excitement for the road! The XKSS was essentially a D-Type fitted with road equipment. To the far left, the dash of the XKSS, while certainly spartan, was still not as primitive as that of a 1954 Le Mans car, near left.

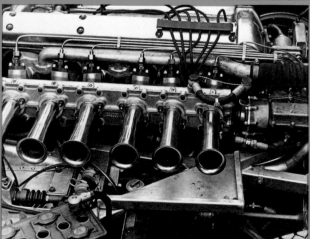

E-TYPE 1

LEAN MACHINE

When the Geneva Salon opened in March of 1961, the visitors were treated to a sight most of them would never forget. Placed by itself, resting on an enormous oriental rug, was a brand-new sports car, with lines so smooth, so sensual, that even the most well-proportioned harem concubine would have been unable to attract more admiring attention.

The occasion was the first public exhibition of the new Jaguar E-Type, and the response was so overwhelming that by the closing of the show, five hundred orders had been taken. Notable British author and car enthusiast, Lord Montague, wrote in one of his Jaguar books about a movie director flying in from Rome, just to place his order; and about a London man, who, upon learning that all the demonstrators were in Geneva, also took to the air, just to be able to test drive one. Such was the impact of Sir William's new masterpiece.

It is arguable which one of Lyons' creations caused the biggest sensation when they were first unveiled—the XK 120, or the E-Type. The XK 120 was certainly both attractive and affordable—so was the E-Type. The latter was acceptable to a larger audience of buyers, especially in its coupe form, which was the only version displayed in Geneva. More acceptable, however, did not mean that the E-Type was less of a sports car. On the contrary, it was closer to an actual racing car—closer in concept than any other mass-produced sports car had ever been, and most likely, would ever be.

When Jaguar bowed out of racing after the 1956 Le Mans, it was not the intention to stay out

for good. The resources of the relatively small company were simply, for the time being, stretched too far. After all, it was in business to produce and sell road cars.

Nevertheless, the competition flame was kept alive within the company. A result of this was a sports racer, referred to as the E2A. It was a development of the D-Type, and was intended for the 1958 Le Mans, should the decision to rejoin the racing scene be made.

The E2A was the link between the D- and the E-Type. It had the smoothed-out, less voluptuous styling of the road car soon to come, although with a higher, somewhat clumbsy-looking rear portion. This alteration was necessitated by the requirement that the car should have room for a certain volume of luggage, as set forth in the rule books. The engine was an aluminum-block, three-liter, fuel-injected version of the XK, producing 293 bhp. Like the future E-Type, it had independent rear suspension, with inboard disc brakes.

Obviously, the E2A was never entered in 1958. It was probably a sound decision to leave a good thing be—it would have taken much more to top the D-Type legend. Although, based on lap times recorded in 1960, when the factory loaned the E2A to the Cunningham team, it would certainly have been capable of beating its competition, had it been raced in 1958. In the hands of Gurney and Hansgen, it posted the fastest lap during practice. In the actual race, however, the car was a disappointment. After having briefly held third position, it dropped to thirty-first after a long pit stop. It gradually rose to ninth place, but after continued problems relating to the fuel-injection system, it had to be withdrawn before the halfway point had been reached.

Simultaneously with the E2A, a first version of the E-Type, the E1A, had also been worked up. This was a scaled-down, aluminum-bodied unit, with a two-and-a-half-liter engine. It was running by late spring of 1958. A second version, built to final scale, was then produced and used

(continued on overleaf)

The shape that caused a sensation! Pictured to the upper left, the E-Type at its premier showing. Visitors to the 1961 Geneva Auto Show inspect it with curiosity and admiration. Above, the interior of an early model. The aluminum dash and console insets, the uncovered glovebox, the square speaker—among many other things—set it apart from later models. Pictured to the lower left, the E2A—a halfway house between the D- and E-Types—during testing at the MIRA track. To the lower right, the same car at Riverside in 1960.

CALIFORNIA
1967 XKE

eldom has the concept of a sports racing car been translated as honestly to a mass-produced sports car as was the case with the E-Type. The heritage of the D-Type, three-time Le Mans winner, is evident in every aspect, from chassis and engine to suspension and styling. This 1967 Survivor, chassis number 1E14206, is virtually unrestored, and belongs to Judith and Bob Gillette, of Long Beach, California.

for extensive testing and development work. Unfortunately, both of these historic prototypes were scrapped by the factory.

Another early morning. Another shooting completed. Above the eastern horizon the sun still hangs low, sending its warming beams of light across the Long Beach harbor with its tankers and tugboats, spreading that primrose-colored light—primrose, like the color of the E-Type standing beside the shore with its engine idling invitingly.

The last shots were of the engine—that most beautiful of all mass-produced engines. Owner Bob Gillette closes the hood and indicates that it's my turn to drive. He bought the car from its original owner in 1976. It's a 1967—the last of the Series One—which is what Bob was specifically looking for, feeling that this version is the most desirable, as it combines the ultimate look of the covered headlights with the improved, all-synchromesh gearbox.

Being back in the cockpit is a nostalgic reunion for me—I once owned an E-Type. All those good, familiar feelings return, awakened by the sound of that instantly recognizable exhaust note, coming crisp and unpretentious from behind; by the sight of that long hood, with its power-evoking bulge; by the feel of the steering wheel; by the tight-fitting seat; and above all, by the feel of that gear lever, positioned right on top of the box—no linkage, no deterioration of communication.

Accelerating past the long, black hull of the Queen Mary, speeding up, crossing the bridge into downtown Long Beach, revving up, shifting, moving out onto an early-morning deserted Shore Line Drive, where the Formula One drivers had battled just a few weeks earlier, my mind sums up all these feelings and produces a conclusive phrase, which it repeats over and over again as the car-and-driver-unit shoots like a bullet through the morning air: There has never been, and will never again be—for the amount of money spent—a more exciting sports car than the E-Type.

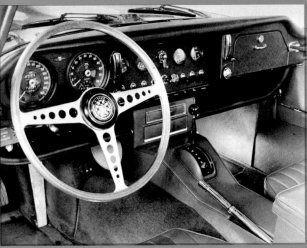

The E-Type Coupe looked unique and exciting from every angle. The only changes one could have wished for—especially with the benefit of hindsight—were a wider track, a less steeply raked windshield, and a lower roofline. In the photos on the opposite page, taken in 1961, the photographer chose very flattering angles to communicate the sensually flowing lines of the Lyons and Sayer masterpiece. With the introduction in 1968 of the 2+2, captured at speed in the picture above, came an alternative for the family with small children. This model had the not-so-sporty automatic option.

E-TYPE 2

SIR WILLIAM'S CHOICE

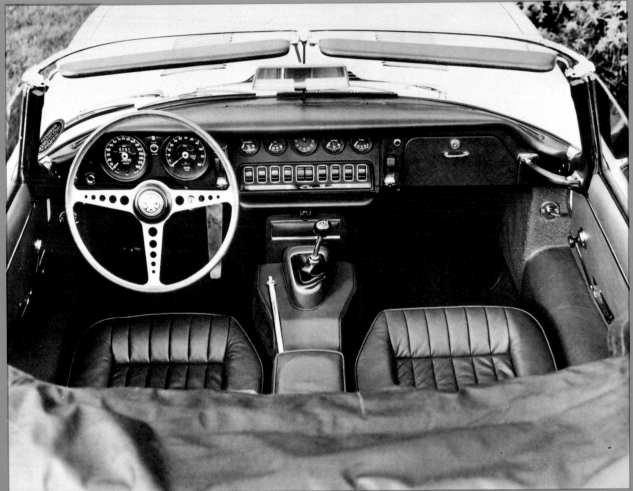

From the viewpoint of styling, the E-Type was the most pure and original design ever to emanate from Jaguar. As has previously been pointed out, both the SS 100 and the XK 120, styled by William Lyons himself, took inspiration from trend setting works by Italian and French coachbuilders. Even the origins of the D-Type, styled by Malcolm Sayer, could be traced to a existing design.

Inspiration for the E-Type, as has been described earlier, came from the D-Type—the heritage is obvious. In the process of translating this shape into a mass-produced street machine, which understandably had to display more generally acceptable lines, Sayer and Lyons managed to create a true piece of art, unique in the world of automotive design.

While the D-Type looked brutish, massive and substantial, the E-Type, with its lean and slender shape, looked more delicate, expressing speed and agility, rather than raw power. The D-Type was certainly the most savagely exciting of the two, while the E-Type was the most pleasingly beautiful.

It is probably correct to assume that Lyons' work sprung from an inborn, spontaneous sense for form, formally uneducated, nevertheless highly refined. The work produced by Malcolm Sayer, on the other hand, had its origin in a functional understanding of form; the parameters of a particular design were set by the laws of aerodynamics, a science he had become well acquainted with while working for the Bristol Aircraft Corporation.

The experience with aircraft manufacture

With the Series Two E-Type, announced in 1968, came a revised interior, seen above. There was safety padding, non-reflective fittings, flush-level handles and switches, break-away steering column and rear-view mirror. Of the exterior revisions, the uncovered lights, the enlarged grille opening and the new indicator lights gave a new look to the front (as seen in the picture above right) while the heavier bumper and the new light cluster (seen to the left) changed the view of the rear. To the right, the increased slant of the windscreen could hardly be noticed without a close comparison.

also affected other aspects of his work. One specific example of this is the dash of the E-Type, with its business like, no-nonsense look. Another example is the use of aircraft-type rivets, as was the case with the D-Type as well as with the E-Type prototypes—all obviously of limited production. For the final, mass-produced product, conventional manufacturing methods were of course employed.

Thanks to Sayer's expertise in the field of aerodynamics, wind-tunnel testing was introduced as a means of judging the efficiency of the new creations. It is interesting to note, however, that Lyons' gut-feeling designs were never far off the mark. In 1953, an XK 120 reached a top speed of 172 mph during a speed record run on a highway in Belgium. This particular car had been fitted with a bubble top and other aerodynamic modifications by Sayer. An interim D-Type, carrying Sayer's first try at the future D-Type shape, managed just sligthly better—178 mph. In fairness, it should be mentioned that the latter car, at this point, was fitted with an engine of smaller displacement.

Still on the subject of aerodynamic efficiency, it may be more accurate to say that none of the shapes referred to were exceptionally efficient. It is, for instance, very likely that the formidable success of the D-Type was not so much a result of its slippery shape, as it was thanks to its light-weight construction. Another example illustrating the fact that the science of aerodynmics was still in an experimental stage in the mid-fifties, is that the XJ-S is said to have attained higher efficiency readings than the D-Type.

Whether the E-Type in roadster form or in coupe form is the most attractive, is certainly a matter of discussion. Both have advantages from a practical viewpoint. The main attraction of the former is of course its convertibility, with the wind-in-the-hair and close-to-nature appeal, while the advantages of the latter of course lie in the fact that it has complete and effective weather protection, as well as im-

(continued on overleaf)

Distinctively unique and seductively rakish, an E-Type Coupe is the quintessential Jaguar, the way a 356 Coupe is the quintessential Porsche. The touch of Lyons, so strikingly evident in the smooth, drop shape of the rear portion, adds visual excitement to this still empty beach walk at dawn. This 1970 Survivor, chassis number 2R28536, belongs to Roberta and Tom Morgan of Rolling Hills Estates, California.

proved luggage-carrying capability. These aspects do not need to be discussed; it is up to each individual to choose the alternative that fits his or her needs.

From the viewpoint of styling, however, the coupe is the quintessential E-Type. The unique lines of the front are complemented and fulfilled by the lines expressed in the roof and tail—both, together, create a most exciting unit. Try the following experiment: Cover the rear half of a side view of the car with your hand; move your hand toward the rear, slowly allowing more and more of the car to become visible, all the time imagining that you do not know what the rear looks like. Would you agree that the effect is most fitting?

While the overall shape of the coupe was unique as a design, the concept was not. Already before the war, there had been both sedans (for instance, Lyons' own Airline Saloon) and sports cars with a streamlined rear. Especially after the war, the Italians seem to have taken a liking to the concept, calling it Berlinetta—which freely translated has come to mean small, fastback sports tourer. Pininfarina's 1947 Cisitalia became a milestone in this respect. Closer to home, Lyons would have been well acquainted with the 1952 Aston Martin DB 2. Pininfarina's 1956 Ferrari Tour de France is perhaps closest to the E-Type theme.

Although a speculative thought, it is nevertheless possible that the coupe configuration was primarily the brain child of Sir William. For the reasons discussed in the previous paragraph, but also for the practical advantages—for Lyons was also a practical man, as evidenced by the not-so-attractive but useful rear-access door—the coupe was an ingenious solution. It is clear that the E-Type was developed as a roadster; as far as the coupe is concerned, it appears to have been an afterthought. Curiously, the only version shown at the Geneva Salon in March of 1961 was the coupe.

The E-Type Coupe—the quintessential E-Type—Sir William's choice?

Shown on these pages, just a few photographs illustrating the enormous scope of the organization Sir William Lyons built—several pages would be needed to give a picture that more justly portrays the various stages of growth and expansion. Above, a scene from the engine testing area as it appeared in 1952. Opposite page, clockwise—all photographs dating from 1964—an aerial view of the Browns Lane Factory. Later, the facilities were enlarged to cover an area of almost twice the size. Administration headquarters are located in the building seen in the foreground. Next, a scene from the new engine testing department. At that time, every unit ran four hours before installation. Then comes the mounting track, where bodies and mechanical components come together. And last, a scene from the final check point. Here the car has returned from a thorough road test, but will yet undergo a final scrutinizing.

E-TYPE 3

THE MAGNIFICENT TWELVE

The early-morning fog hangs heavy over the landscape, covering the grassy field and the low hills that surround the setting like the grandstands of a football stadium. I had found the location the previous afternoon, at that time considering it excellent because of those hills blocking out houses and power lines and all other reminders of human presence. I wanted just one such presence—the car to be photographed. But now, because of that thick fog, those hills don't matter anymore. I'm in trouble; looking through the lens I can hardly see the car, much less the hills.

Nearly a decade had passed since the last great Jaguar victory at Le Mans, and once again there was activity in the experimental division; early in 1966, a beautifully streamlined machine had been tested in extreme secrecy, reaching almost 180 mph on the straightaways of the MIRA track. Not only did this machine, with its purposeful lines, have the looks of a serious contender, it also carried a most formidable power unit inside its belly—the embryo of Jaguar's future V-12.

Begun already in 1955, when it was felt that Jaguar needed a new engine in order to be competitive at Le Mans, it would take until 1964 before the first unit was ready for the test bed. This long delay was the result of Jaguar's on-and-off racing policy. The factory was in fact never again fully committed to racing, not the way it had once been. With production resources stretched to the limit, there was never enough capacity, nor incentive.

The XK unit was intended for road use; its fitness for racing was an attractive side benefit.

Although Jaguars always came with a comparatively low price tag, the standard of creature comfort was never compromised, as the pictures on these pages testify. Above, a portion of the 420 dash. Wood was always present in ample quantities, as was leather. Left, the dash of the original edition XJ6. Lower right, the dash of the 1973 Series Two model. Note the increase in size of the steering wheel padding. Above right, the sumptuous cockpit of the XJ-S, here seen as it looked at introduction in 1976.

The V-12, on the other hand, was planned for a dual role, road and racing units being developed simultaneously. At the initial test bed runs, the former produced around 300 bhp, while the latter supplied 500 bhp.

This marvelous V-12, with its twin set of double overhead cams, was all a racing enthusiast could ever have asked for. And not only were the technical specifications overwhelming, its physical appearance, too, was awe inspiring. Unfortunately, it never saw competition; in 1967, the Jaguar company joined hands with BMC, and with this amalgamation came yet another change in priorities.

Fortunately, this did not mean the end of the efforts to develop a road-going V-12. A combination of factors led to the continued work with this particular type of engine. One of these factors was the perfect interior balance inherent in this configuration. Another was its exotic image.

In its final form, the double overhead cams were not retained. This arrangement was too bulky—a modern car needs an array of auxiliary equipment, and there was simply not enough room. Imagine the original unit, with its massive but clean exterior, shoe-horned into the E-Type—what a sight! Instead, regrettably, the under-hood picture of the production V-12, with the confusion of plumbing, wiring and shielding, did not look pretty.

Nevertheless, the V-12 was a masterpiece, and every reporter sang its praise. Paul Frere, for one, wrote in Motor: I am pleased to be able to say that none of the exotics I drove during this period—most of them costing nearly twice as much—could claim to have an engine of equal overall merit.

Gordon Liechti, the owner of the Series Three E-Type that now begins to show vaguely in my lens, stands off to the side, arms crossed in a thoughtful pose. He gazes at the shapes that become more and more defined.

Gordon bought the car in 1981, while living in

(continued on overleaf)

W hile the flared fenders and the wider tires bestowed an awesome new look upon the old shapes, the splendid V-12 gave awesome new power, delaying the inevitable end of the E-Type era. The perfectly restored 1973 Series 3 captured in these photographs has chassis number 1S21433, and belongs to Gordon Liechty of Lake Forest, California.

Oregon. Having gained an interest in British cars through first an MG Midget, then a Triumph TR6, he was ready to move up to a Jaguar. Well, he had been ready all along, but funds had always been the problem. Now, at the age of twenty-four, he was finally able to fulfill his desire.

His choice was the top-of-the-line E-Type, the one featuring the magnificent V-12. The combination of white and black was a prerequisite, as was the early small-bumper version. The example he finally found, was pretty run down, the paint faded, the seats torn, the engine extremely tired. However, he gradually began improving its condition, at this point unaware of how far he would ultimately go. A visit to the Forest Grove Concourse opened his eyes.

He went at the task with determination, disassembling the entire car, labeling the parts, placing them in bags, making notes and drawing diagrams to help with the future reassembly. Most of the engine rebuilding was done by himself, while painting and upholstering was left to appropriate specialists.

Well aware that a project of this nature is a never-ending undertaking, he nevertheless entered the completed car in the 1984 Jaguar Club Concourse in San Diego—just to see where he stood. An honorable third in class was the reward. Now he is refining it further, working on the all-important details.

Looking through the lens, I find that the sun is burning off more and more of the fog, its density now appearing just right. I motion for Gordon to turn on the headlights. I check the effect. The boldness of the massive Jaguar fills the frame with its presence. And with the lights blazing, it becomes even more awesome. I decide I was lucky about the fog after all—surrounded by this miracle of nature, isolated, the magnificence of the man-made object is now even more intriguingly expressed than I had originally hoped for. It stands as a miracle of a different kind, a symbol of man's ingenuity, a monument to his quest for perfection.

The Series Three E-Type conquers Newport Beach! The longer wheelbase and the wider track, the bigger tires—necessitating the introduction of flares—the larger cockpit, the wider doors, the new grille—all added up to a much improved car. It was nevertheless greeted with ambiguity when introduced in 1971. Sure, it was better than before, but it was still old fashioned, according to the motor magazines. Sure, it looked bold and capable, but something of that classic E-Type sleekness had been lost. What saved the day was the magnificent V-12, it gave the Series Three the status of an instant classic.

LEAVING
A LEGACY

For the Jaguar Company, the year of 1972 was one of milestones. Incredible as it seemed, fifty years had passed since that day in the early-twenties, when William Lyons, together with his partner William Walmsley, put his signature to the agreement that launched the Swallow Sidecar Company. Now, at the age of seventy-one, Lyons was certainly still vigorous. It was only when one remembered how young he had been at the outset of his career, that those fifty years could be fathomed. During the first months in 1922, before young William had reached the legal age of twenty-one, the company checks actually had to be countersigned by his father.

The official celebration of the fiftieth anniversary took place on Lyons' birthday, the fourth of September. He had in fact retired earlier in the year, relinquishing his duties as Chairman of the Board and Chief Executive of Jaguar Cars. In October, as a final act—signifying the end of the Lyons era—the company became a part of British Leyland.

However, before retiring, Lyons had taken steps to ensure that the cars produced by the new organization would carry his personal signature for a long time to come. The new saloon, the XJ6, had been introduced in 1968. It was universally praised, both for its styling as well as for its engineering. Road & Track, for instance, included it in its selection of the World's Ten Best Cars. More importantly, the buying public agreed with the journalists, making 1971 the year of a new production record—total annual output passed the 32,000-unit mark for the first time.

The styling of the XJ-S was not an altogether pleasing affair. First of all, it seemed to deviate too much from the classic Jaguar themes—only the frontal view, as seen to the left, and the low roof contributed some continuity. Otherwise, it seemed to have elements from certain Italian exotics. Above, the European version, with single-unit headlights. These were much more flattering than the double units of the US version, and harmonized with the design theme evident in the rear lights. Despite initial doubts, the XJ-S has earned a place of its own among the world's great touring machines.

The last project to receive Lyons' attention, was the XJ-S. Although the finished product did not reach the marketplace until 1975, development work had begun in the late-sixties. By the early-seventies, just before Sir William's retirement, the styling phase of the new car had been completed.

As with the E-Type, Lyons again worked with Malcolm Sayer, although it is obvious that the latter did most of the work. It is also possible, by now, with Lyons ready to retire, that the influence of other forces had their effect. Sir William has stated that he purposely let aerodynamic requirements, as set forth by Sayer, take precedence over individual taste considerations. This might account for the fact that the XJ-S does not seem to follow Jaguar tradition. It is mainly the front, with its headlights and grille (reminiscent of an XJ6 study Lyons created in the mid-sixties), together with the comparatively low windscreen and the compact roofline (as seen on a mid-fifties study for a XK 140 replacement), that are evidence of the fact that Lyons indeed had a hand in the styling.

Otherwise, the effect of the overall shape—although certainly unique—was rather mixed up, displaying elements similar to those found on certain Italian exotics of the mid-sixties. The hood, for instance, is reminiscent of Lamborghini's 400 GT, and the tail butresses seem to have been lifted from Ferrari's Dino.

Thus the new model was received with mixed emotions. The primary reason for this was certainly the fact that it was not a replacement for the E-Type, as Jaguar enthusiasts had hoped for. Second, as we have seen above, the styling was not as sensational as one had come to expect from Jaguar. Once these initial reactions had been assimilated, however, a feeling of respect began to take their place. For, bearing in mind its concept of luxurious grand touring machine as opposed to bare-essentials sports car and, as always with a Jaguar, considering value for money spent, the XJ-S admittedly was in a class by itself.

(continued on overleaf)

Seldom has a model been more eagerly awaited than the XJ-S. If, upon unveiling, there was a whisper of disappointment, it was only because the XJ-S was not a sports car—not a replacement for the E-Type. Certainly, for what it is, an exceptionally comfortable, luxurious and fast touring machine, the XJ-S has succeeded in carving out a place for itself among the great cars of today. The example featured in these photographs a 1983 model, chassis number 2DC111036, belongs to Chic Vandagriff of Hollywood, California.

With the new products in place, and with a new partnership to carry on what he had begun, the future seemed secure, and Sir William could allow his life to take on a less regimented routine, although it was not one of idleness. He continued to stay abreast of developments both inside the company as well as within the automotive world as a whole. However, he now had time to develop another area of interest, sheep farming. He applied his rational mind to this field as well, and Wappenbury Hall, the large estate he had owned since the late twenties, became a model of efficiency—just as his company had been.

It is ample testimony to the genius of William Lyons that more than a decade after his retirement, the company is still earning its livelihood from the models he created. Although, for a while, the organization suffered from the loss of its founder's strong influence. During this time Jaguar hit a low point, with respect to its reputation for quality and reliability. After a string of top executives, the post as Chairman of the Board was given to John Egan. Under his leadership, Jaguar has returned to its former greatness, quality control being of the foremost concern. This has resulted in a phenomenal increase in sales; Jaguars are now once again just as difficult to obtain as they were during Sir William's days at the helm.

Wappenbury Hall, February 8, 1985. There's an erie stillness over the entire estate this morning. Even the manor house stands quiet, as if in reverence. The chimneys, the roofs, the windows, the verandas—all elements of a timeless design—suddenly show their age. The Master, usually awake at this hour, often getting ready for an inspection tour of his herd, is nowhere to be seen. Down by the road, the massive gate, stretched between great, formal columns, is closed. The flow of cars, so many of them Sir William's own creations, has stopped. Even his personal Daimler Sovereign stands cold in its garage...

Featured on these pages are various applications of Jaguar's V-12 engine. Top of opposite page, near right, the beginning of it all! The year was 1964, and the company was toying with the idea of returning to Le Mans. In fact this had been an off-and-on proposition since the mid-fifties, when the V-12 project was first begun. As can be seen, at this point the twin sets of double overhead cams were still employed. In racing trim, the unit developed 500 bhp. Above, and far right, two racing applications of the final product. First, as mounted in the 1974 Group 44 E-Type, so successfully campaigned by Bob Tullius. Second, as fitted in two 1976 XJ12 Coupes, prepared for the European Championship for Touring Cars. Left, as introduced in the XJ12. Right, as fitted to the Series Three E-Type. In both applications, carburetors were used. To the far right, as mounted in the XJ-S, now fuel-injected.

JAGUARS FOR THE ROAD

THE SURVIVORS SERIES

Jaguars for the Road,
tenth in The Survivors Series,
was photographed, designed,
written by Henry Rasmussen.
Assistant designer was Walt
Woesner. Copy editor, Barbara
Harold. Tintype Graphic Arts
of San Luis Obispo, California,
supplied the typesetting.
The color separations, as well
as the printing and binding,
were produced by South China
Printing Company in Hong
Kong. Liaison with the printer
was Peter Lawrence.

The black and white pictures
were mainly obtained from
the library of Road & Track,
where Otis Meyer provided
valuable help.

Special acknowledgements go
to Bill Kosfeld of Motorbooks
International for his capable and
pleasant handling of all the
various matters connected with
publishing; and, again, to Tom
Warth, president of Motorbooks
International, whose continued
support makes it all possible.

In addition to the owners
of the featured automobiles, the
author also wishes to thank
Chuck Albee, Bruce Carnahan,
Ken Van Doren, Ed Erskine,
Joseph Fredericks, James Groth,
Walter Hill, Holly Hollenbeck,
Ray Lewis, Mark Mayuga, Roy
Miller, Ray Nierlich, Steve
Roberts, Ray Sanches, Robert
Sheehee, George Sirus, Don,
Watts, and Don Zweifel.